Resolution in Europe: The Unresolved Questions

Institute for Law and Finance Series

Edited by
Theodor Baums
Andreas Cahn

Volume 22

Resolution in Europe: The Unresolved Questions

Edited by
Andreas Dombret
Patrick S. Kenadjian

DE GRUYTER

ISBN 978-3-11-064021-2
e-ISBN (PDF) 978-3-11-064406-7
e-ISBN (EPUB) 978-3-11-064050-2

Library of Congress Control Number: 2018967847

Bibliografische Information der Deutschen Nationalbibliothek
Die Deutsche Nationalbibliothek verzeichnet diese Publikation in der Deutschen Nationalbibliografie; detaillierte bibliografische Daten sind im Internet über http://dnb.d-nb.de abrufbar.

Typesetting: Integra Software Services Pvt. Ltd.
Printing and binding: CPI books GmbH, Leck
Cover image: Medioimages/Photodisc

www.degruyter.com

Introduction

On April 23, 2018, the Institute for Law and Finance at the Goethe University, Frankfurt am Main hosted the fourth in a series of day-long conferences on the subject of "too big to fail", the problem which has generally been acknowledged to be the key legacy of the great financial crisis of 2008/2009. When the ILF held the first of this series of conferences in November 2010, the goal was to introduce what was then a relatively unknown concept to Germany, that of bank resolution, so we resorted to the somewhat tortured title of "Brauchen wir ein Sonderinsolvenzrecht für Banken?", do we need a special insolvency law for banks? At that time, Germany was considering adjusting its insolvency laws and our goal was to explain the advantages of an administrative resolution proceeding over traditional insolvency laws in the case of financial institutions. Interestingly enough, while resolution has since been widely accepted as the right approach for failing financial institutions, the idea that national insolvency laws should also be adjusted to the needs of the bank insolvencies is making a comeback, not only in the United States with current proposals for a new Chapter 14 of the U.S. Bankruptcy Code, but also in Europe, as the difficulties of applying a uniform EU approach to resolution sitting atop differing member state laws is becoming more apparent.

The ILF's second bite at the too big to fail question came in May 2012 as Europe was awaiting the European Commission's release of its draft of what became the Bank Recovery and Resolution Directive and represented an attempt to focus on targeting what participants saw as the key points the Commission needed to address. Many of the published contributions to the book which resulted from the conference also provided a first critique of the Commission's draft.

The ILF's third approach to the too big to fail problem came in January 2014 when we examined whether the real solution of the problem should come not from bank resolution, but from actually breaking up the banks. The majority of the participants at the conference concluded that the various models then on offer for breaking up the banks as embodied in the Volcker Rule in the U.S. and the recommendations of the Vickers Report in the U.K. and of the Liikanen Report in the EU, did not present convincingly superior solutions to resolution, especially since the recovery and resolution plan mechanisms embodied in resolution allow the banks and their supervisors to develop tailored approaches to splitting up particular banking groups in case of failure rather than a "one size fits all" approach prescribed by the statutory solutions.

We revisited the issue again in April 2018, this time not to debate new proposals for tackling the problem but, in accordance with the temper of the times, to evaluate whether the course we have adopted so far is "fit for purpose".

https://doi.org/10.1515/9783110644067-201

Our focus was on Europe and our goal to determine whether the problem has been solved or remains, partly, if not largely, unresolved. While our geographical focus narrowed, our scope widened. Heretofore our sessions had concentrated largely on bank resolution, leaving to one side insurance companies and central counterparties ("CCPs"). Insurance companies in liquidation, said to be "in run-off mode", have traditionally been represented to be extremely stable, since they incur no new liabilities and simply use their existing assets to pay off obligations as they mature. This may be right to the extent insurance companies confine themselves to writing traditional insurance, but once they begin to write derivatives and become asset managers, the possibility that they may need a resolution regime cannot be ignored, as we learned from the problems of AIG and the mono line insurers during the great financial crisis.

CCPs are unique in the resolution universe in that while banks and insurance companies have in a sense "always been with us" and their problems were evident in the great financial crisis, CCPs in their current form and importance are a creation and consequence of that crisis, specifically of the rules adopted to reduce counterparty risk by requiring central clearing of derivatives. They are also unique in that, in contrast to banks and insurance companies, which are large institutions, with assets and liabilities susceptible of being restructured along traditional lines, a failing CCP is a relatively small place with a failed risk model and not much to restructure.

The conference concluded that, while significant progress had been made on bank resolution, there remained work to be done in implementing many of its procedures and harmonizing national approaches across the European Union, as well as additional work to ensure that the proper structures and incentives are in place to promote cooperation in cross-border resolution. The conference also showed that much less progress had been made on insurance company resolution, that more work needs to be done in this area and that the approach may need to be different from that taken with banks. With respect to CCPs, we seem to be closer to the beginning of the discussion, with the realization that while recovery plans are local in nature, developed by the national resolution authority in the country where the CCP is physically located, the effect of the failure of a CCP would have consequences well beyond the jurisdiction where the CCP is located, through losses suffered by clearing members organized elsewhere and that, given how CCPs are capitalized and structured, the need for recourse to taxpayer money in case of a CCP failure cannot at this time be excluded, an issue which clearly needs more attention.

Andreas Dombret
Patrick Kenadjian

Frankfurt am Main July 2018

Contents

The Authors

José Manuel Campa

José Manuel Campa, holds a Ph.D. and a master degree in economics from Harvard University. Currently, he is Professor of Financial Management and International Economics at the University of Navarra-IESE.

Between 2009 and 2011 Campa served as Secretary of State for the Economy in the Ministry of Economy and Finances of Spain, a position that allowed him to be one of the heads of the Spanish economy in times of great responsibility. He specializes in international finance and macroeconomics and has been professor of strategy and financial management courses in financial institutions like Goldman Sachs, Citibank, ABN Amro, BBVA and Santander.

Mr. Campa has also been a consultant to a large number of international organizations, including the International Monetary Fund, the Inter-American Development Bank, the Bank of International Settlements in Basel, and the European Commission. He currently serves in the Expert Group, chair by Mr. Erkki Liikanen, evaluating policy recommendations on structural reforms for the European Banking industry.

He has also taught at the Stern School of Business of New York University; Harvard University; and at Columbia University. He has been Research Associate at the National Bureau of Economic Research and Research Fellow at the Center for Economic Policy Research and is a member of the board of Bruegel. He has also served as an expert for the Spanish justice, at the Spanish Court of Arbitration, and at international courts of arbitration in Paris, Geneva, New York and the Netherlands.

Benoît Cœuré

Benoît Cœuré has been a member of the Executive Board of the European Central Bank since 1 January 2012. He is responsible for International and European Relations, Market Operations and the Oversight of Payment Systems. He is the Chairman of the Committee on Payments and Market Infrastructures (CPMI) of the Bank for International Settlements, and has held this position since October 2013.

Prior to joining the ECB, he served in various policy positions at the French Treasury. He was the Deputy Chief Executive, then Chief Executive, of the French debt management office, Agence France Trésor, between 2002 and 2007. From 2007 to 2009, he was France's Assistant Secretary for Multilateral Affairs, Trade and Development. From 2009 to 2011, he was Deputy Director General and Chief Economist of the French Treasury.

https://doi.org/10.1515/9783110644067-202

Mr Cœuré is a graduate of the École polytechnique in Paris. He holds an advanced degree in statistics and economic policy from the École nationale de la statistique et de l'administration économique (ENSAE) and a B.A. in Japanese. He is an affiliate professor at Sciences Po in Paris. He has authored articles and books on economic policy, the international monetary system and the economics of European integration, including *Dealing with the New Giants: Rethinking the Role of Pension Funds* (CEPR, 2006, with Tito Boeri, Lans Bovenberg and Andrew Roberts) and *Economic Policy: Theory and Practice* (Oxford University Press, Second Edition, 2018, with Agnès Bénassy-Quéré, Pierre Jacquet and Jean Pisani-Ferry).

Dr Andreas Dombret

Dr Andreas Dombret was born in the USA to German parents. He studied business management at the Westfälische Wilhelms University in Münster and was awarded his PhD by the Friedrich-Alexander University in Erlangen-Nuremberg.

From 1987 to 1991, he worked at Deutsche Bank's Head Office in Frankfurt, from 1992 to 2002 at JP Morgan in Frankfurt and London, from 2002 to 2005 as the Co-Head of Rothschild Germany located in Frankfurt and London, before serving Bank of America as Vice Chairman for Europe and Head for Germany, Austria and Switzerland between 2005 and 2009. He was awarded an honorary professorship from the European Business School in Oestrich-Winkel in 2009.

From May 2010 to May 2018, he has been a member of the Executive Board of the Deutsche Bundesbank with responsibility for Financial Stability, Statistics, Markets, Banking and Financial Supervision, Economic Education, Risk Controlling and the Bundesbank's Representative Offices abroad. He was also responsible for the IMF (Deputy of the Bundesbank), Financial Stability Commission (Member), Supervisory Board of the SSM (Member), Basel Committee on Banking Supervision (BCBS) (Member) and is still a member of the Board of Directors at the Bank for International Settlements, Basel.

D. Wilson Ervin

Vice Chairman Group Executive Office, Credit Suisse Group AG

Mr. Ervin is a Vice Chairman at Credit Suisse in the group executive office. He works on a variety of strategic projects, especially policy reforms related to bank capital and ending "too-big-to-fail". He also chairs the Credit Suisse Americas Foundation and the Impact Investment Advisory Council.

Prior to his current role, Mr. Ervin was the Chief Risk Officer of Credit Suisse, a member of the Executive Board, and chair of the Capital Allocation and Risk Management Committee. From 1990 to 1998, Mr. Ervin worked at

Credit Suisse Financial Products, where he headed new product development. Before 1990, he held various roles in capital markets (both fixed income & equity), Australia investment banking and the Mergers & Acquisitions group.

Mr. Ervin recently received the Risk Magazine "Lifetime Achievement Award" for his efforts to end "too big to fail" and Bail-in. He received his A.B., summa cum laude, in economics from Princeton University.

Joachim Faber

Joachim Faber has been Chairman of the Supervisory Board of Deutsche Boerse since May 2012 and a member of its Supervisory Board since May 2009. He has also been an independent non-executive director of HSBC since March 2012. He has a background in banking and asset management with significant international experience, having worked in Germany, Tokyo, New York and London.

Mr Faber was formerly Chief Executive Officer of Allianz Global Investors AG and a member of the management board of Allianz SE. He is an independent director of Coty Inc. and a director of Allianz France SA, as well as the Chairman of the Shareholder Committee of Joh A Benckiser SARL and the supervisory board of Deutsche Boerse AG. He is also a member of the advisory board of the European School for Management and Technology and council member of the Hong Kong-Europe Business Council.

He has 14 years' experience with Citigroup Inc., holding positions in Trading and Project Finance and as Head of Capital Markets for Europe, North America and Japan. He holds a law degree from Bonn University and has a doctorate from the German University of Administrative Sciences in Speyer.

Adam Farkas

Adam Farkas is the first Executive Director of the European Banking Authority (EBA). He was appointed in March 2011 and is serving his second five-year term.

Prior to this appointment, Adam Farkas served as Chairman of the Hungarian Financial Supervisory Authority. He started his career as an Assistant Professor at the Budapest University of Economic Sciences. He has also been a consultant to various financial institutions in Budapest and London, including the European Bank for Reconstruction and Development (EBRD). He became Managing Director and Member of the Board at the National Bank of Hungary where he was responsible, among other things, for reserve management, open market operations, treasury, and government banking services. He also worked in the private sector as co-CEO of CIB Bank

Ltd. a subsidiary of the Intesa Group and later as CEO of Allianz Bank Ltd. (Allianz Group).

Prof. Dr. Helmut Gründl

After his postdoctoral lecture qualification ("Habilitation") at the University of Passau, Prof. Gründl was Professor at Humboldt University Berlin from 1999 until 2010, before he moved to Goethe University Frankfurt in 2010 where he holds the Chair of Insurance and Regulation and serves as Managing Director of the International Center for Insurance Regulation (ICIR).

Prof. Gründl's main research interests lie in the area of insurance, insurance regulation and risk management. He has worked on the question of policyholders' demand behavior under the possible risk of forgoing insurance benefits and on the resulting consequences for the regulation of insurance companies. Presently his research focuses on insurance regulation in order to strengthen the scientific basis for regulatory decisions.

In his quantitatively oriented lectures he covers corporate finance, insurance economics, and the asset and liability management of insurance companies.

Dr. Levin Holle

Director General, Financial Markets Policy Department, Federal Ministry of Finance, Berlin, Germany

Levin Holle is the Head of the Financial Markets Policy Department of Germany's Federal Ministry of Finance. His responsibilities include the formulation of policies and strategies with respect to federal credit institutions, federal debt management, financial markets as well as anti-money laundering and international financial markets policy. He is also responsible for the supervision of the Federal Financial Supervisory Authority and the Financial Market Stabilisation Authority. Additionally he is supervisory board member of the Deutsche Bahn AG since 2018.

Prior to joining the German Finance Ministry he worked 15 years for the management consultancy Boston Consulting Group, his last position being Senior Partner and Managing Director of the Berlin office. In 1996 he earned his Ph.D. at the University of Göttingen.

Dr. Thomas F. Huertas

Dr. Thomas F. Huertas is currently a Senior Fellow at the Center for Financial Studies and an Adjunct Professor at the Institute of Law and Finance (both at the Goethe University Frankfurt). Until June 2018 Tom was a partner in the risk practice at EY where he chaired the firm's Global Regulatory Network and advised major financial institutions on regulatory and strategic issues. Prior to joining EY at the start of 2012 Dr. Huertas was a Member of the Executive Committee at the UK Financial Services Authority and Alternate Chair of the European Banking Authority. He also served as a member of the Basel Committee on Banking Supervision and as a member of the Resolution Steering Committee at the Financial Stability Board. Prior to joining the FSA in 2004, Tom held a number of senior positions at Citigroup as well as the CEO role at Orbian, an internet-based supply chain finance company.

In addition to his university roles, Tom acts as a non-executive director for Barclays Bank Ireland. He holds a Ph.D. in Economics from the University of Chicago and has published extensively on financial regulation.

Felix Hufeld

Felix Hufeld is President of the German Federal Financial Supervisory Authority (BaFin). Previously he was Chief Executive Director Insurance Supervision at BaFin. Before he was Partner at Westlake Partners. From 2001 to 2010 he served as Chief Executive Officer of Marsh Germany, Austria and Northern Europe of Marsh & Mclennan Companies Inc. Prior to joining the insurance sector, Felix Hufeld worked from 1999 to 2001 at Dresdner Bank as their Global Head Group Corporate Development. Prior to that, he worked at The Boston Consulting Group (BCG) for almost eight years, in the end as a Principal, primarily focusing on the financial services industry as well as attorney focusing on corporate and tax law.

Felix Hufeld studied law in Freiburg and received a Master in Public Administration at Harvard University.

Felix Hufeld is member of the Supervisory Board of the Single Supervisory Mechanism (SSM) of the European Central Bank (ECB) and of the Group of Governors and Heads of Supervision (GHOS), the oversight body of the Basel Committee on Banking Supervision (BCBS), as well as of the Global Financial Stability Board (FSB).

Patrick Kenadjian
Senior Counsel, Davis Polk & Wardwell LLP

Patrick is currently an Adjunct Professor at the Goethe University in Frankfurt am Main, Germany, where he teaches courses on the financial crisis and financial reform and mergers and acquisitions at the Institute for Law and Finance.

Patrick has chaired conferences at the Goethe University in Frankfurt on bank culture and ethics, the EU's Capital Markets Initiative, "too big to fail", the EU's Bank Recovery and Resolution Directive and the EU's

Collective Action Clause initiative and sovereign debt restructuring. He speaks frequently on topics related to financial reform, including "too big to fail," the architecture of financial supervision and the new regulatory environment in the US and the EU. He has acted as Program Director for the Salzburg Global Seminar's Finance in a Changing World Series in 2013 and 2014 and is currently a member of its Advisory Committee.

Patrick is also Senior Counsel at Davis Polk & Wardwell London LLP. He was a partner of the firm from 1984 to 2010, during which time he opened the firm's Tokyo and Frankfurt offices in 1987 and 1991, respectively and spent over 25 years in its European and Asian offices. He speaks French, German and Italian.

He has been listed as a leading lawyer in several industry publications, including *Chambers Global: The World's Leading Lawyers for Business and Legal Media Group's Expert Guide to the World's Leading Banking Lawyers, Expert Guide to the World's Leading Capital Markets Lawyers and Expert Guide to the World's Leading Lawyers Best of the Best*."

Elke König
Chair of the Single Resolution Board
Dr Elke König is Chair of the SRB, being responsible for the management of the organisation, the work of the Board, the budget, all staff, and the Executive and Plenary sessions of the Board. The General Counsel, the Policy Coordination and International Relations Unit, the Communications office and the Internal Audit function report directly to her.

She was President of the German Federal Financial Supervisory Authority (Bundesanstalt für Finanzdienstleistungsaufsicht, BaFin) from 2012 until 2015. After qualifying in business administration and obtaining a doctorate, Dr König spent many years working for companies in the financial and insurance sector. From 1980 to 1990, she worked for KPMG Deutsche Treuhandgesellschaft in Cologne, auditing and advising insurance undertakings, from 1986 as a holder of a special statutory authority (Prokuristin) and from 1988 as a director and partner. From 1990 to 2002, Dr König was a member of the senior management of the Munich Re Group (Head of Accounting); she then moved to Hannover Rückversicherung AG as Chief Financial Officer. From 2010 to the end of 2011, Dr König was a member of the International Accounting Standards Board (IASB) in London. Dr König was also a representative of the Supervisory Board of the Single Supervisory Mechanism.

Daniel Maguire
Chief Executive Officer, LCH Group

Daniel was appointed Chief Executive Officer of LCH Group in October 2017. Prior to being appointed as CEO, Daniel was most recently Group COO. Daniel joined LCH in 1999, and during his 16-year career at LCH, Daniel has had involvement in, and responsibility for, risk management, default management, product management, regulatory strategy, programme delivery, sales, marketing and operations across LCH's SwapClear service, chairing SwapClear Default Management Group and taking part in LCH Risk Committee. In 2014, after returning from four years in the US, where he started and built out LCH's North America operations and led SwapClear's client clearing franchise, Daniel took on the role of Global Head of SwapClear and subsequently took responsibility for LCH's ForexClear and Listed Rates services, and the initiation of LCH's SwapAgent service. Daniel worked at JPMorgan from 2005 to 2008 before returning to LCH on 1 September 2008, where he was immediately responsible for the successful trading and unwinding of Lehman Brothers' LCH-cleared bond and repo portfolio.

In these functions, Daniel has been able to make significant contributions to the development of CCP and derivatives regulatory frameworks across the globe (DFA, EMIR etc.) since the financial crisis. Daniel was appointed to the Board of the International Swaps and Derivatives Association Inc. (ISDA) in April 2018, and is also a member of London Stock Exchange Group's Executive Committee.

Steven Maijoor

Steven Maijoor has been the Chair of the European Securities and Markets Authority (ESMA) since taking up office 1 April 2011. He is the first chair of the authority and is currently serving his second five-year term. He is responsible for representing the Authority as well as chairing ESMA's Board of Supervisors and the Management Board. The role of the Board of Supervisors is to give strategic guidance to ESMA and make all main regulatory and supervisory decisions. The Management Board's purpose is to ensure that the Authority carries out its mission and performs its tasks.

Prior to taking up this role, Steven was Managing Director at the AFM, the Dutch financial markets regulator, where he was responsible for capital market supervision, including financial reporting and auditing, prospectuses, public offerings, and the supervision of the integrity of financial markets. During his term, the scope of activities of the AFM vastly expanded and he was responsible for building and implementing supervision in the capital market area. In his regulatory role at the AFM, Steven has held a number of international positions, including the Chairmanship of IFIAR (International Forum of Independent Audit Regulators).

Before joining the regulatory world, Steven was the Dean of the School of Business and Economics at Maastricht University, and had pursued a long career in academia which included a variety of positions at Maastricht University and the University of Southern California.

He holds a PhD in Business Economics from Maastricht University, was a research student at the London School of Economics, and has a master in Business Economics from the University of Groningen.

Fausto Parente
Executive Director, European Insurance and Occupational Pensions Authority (EIOPA)
Fausto Parente is the Executive Director of the European Insurance and Occupational Pensions Authority (EIOPA). In his role, he presides over the day-to-day management of EIOPA. Mr Parente was elected by the Board of Supervisors of EIOPA on 28 January 2016. His nomination followed an open selection procedure and a public hearing at the European Parliament's Committee on Economic and Monetary Affairs. On 9 March 2016 the European Parliament confirmed his appointment. Mr Parente has a distinguished career in supervisory regulations and policies at national and international level. Prior to his current role he was Head of the Supervisory Regulation and Policy Directorate at the Italian Insurance Supervisor, IVASS – Istituto di Vigilanza sulle Assicurazioni.

He was the Alternate Member in EIOPA Board of Supervisors and member of the Advisory Technical Committee of the European Systemic Risk Board (ESRB). In the context of the Italian Chairmanship in the EU Council (second half of 2014), Mr Parente chaired the Council's working group on Insurance Mediation Directive negotiations. In 2011–2016 he chaired the Insurance Group Supervision Committee of EIOPA and in 2015–2016 - the Joint ESAs Committee on Financial Conglomerates. For several years he was an alternate member in the Technical and Financial Stability Committees of the International Association of Insurance Supervisors (IAIS).

Mr Parente has a degree in Economics from the University Federico II, Naples, and he is graduated to practice as a certified accountant and financial analyst. He has attended many post-graduate courses in the fields of management, European Community law, economy and finance of insurance undertakings. He is author of a series of publications on insurance supervision.

Giulio Terzariol

Mr. Giulio Terzariol has been Chief Financial Officer and Member of Management Board of Allianz SE since January 1, 2018 and served as its Head of Group Planning and Controlling since January 1, 2016. Mr. Terzariol served as the Chief Financial Officer and Treasurer of Allianz Life Insurance Company of New York from October 20, 2008 to December 31, 2015. He served as the Chief Financial Officer, Senior Vice President and Treasurer of Allianz Life Insurance Company of North America, Inc. from July 16, 2008 to December 31, 2015. He was responsible to lead all financial functions at Allianz Life including financial planning, management, and reporting and corporate risk management. He served as Business Financial Officer of Allianz Life Insurance Company of North America from 2007 to July 2008 where, he was responsible for financial planning, business performance management and financial governance. He joined Allianz SE in 1998 as a Financial Analyst after working in international training programs for the Generali Group. He held various leadership positions in Group Planning and Controlling. He served as Regional Chief Financial Officer of Allianz Asia Pacific, based in Singapore. He has been a Director of Allianz Life Insurance Company of North America since August 01, 2008. He served as Director of Allianz Life Insurance Company of New York from April 28, 2009 to December 31, 2015. Mr. Terzariol earned his Bachelor degree in Finance and Business Administration from University L. Bocconi in Milan, Italy.

Paul Tucker

Sir Paul Tucker is chair of the Systemic Risk Council, a fellow at Harvard Kennedy School, and author of *Unelected Power: The Quest for Legitimacy in Central Banking and the Regulatory State* (Princeton University Press). His other activities include being a director at Swiss Re, a senior fellow at the Harvard Center for European Studies, a Visiting Fellow of Nuffield College Oxford, a member of the Advisory Board of the Yale Program on Financial Stability, and a Governor of the Ditchley Foundation. Previously, he was Deputy Governor at the Bank of England, sitting on its monetary policy, financial stability, and prudential policy committees. Internationally, he was a member of the G20 Financial Stability Board, chairing its group on too big to fail; and a director of the Bank for International Settlements, chairing its Committee on Payment and Settlement Systems.

James von Moltke

James von Moltke is the Chief Financial Officer and member of the Management Board of Deutsche Bank since July 1, 2017. Before joining Deutsche Bank, he served as Treasurer of Citigroup, managing its capital and funding as well as liquidity and interest rate risk. He started his career at Credit Suisse First Boston in London in 1992. In 1995, he joined J.P. Morgan, working at the bank for 10 years in New York and Hong Kong. After working at Morgan Stanley for four years, where he led the Financial Technology advisory team globally, James von Moltke joined Citigroup as Head of Corporate M&A in 2009. Three years later he became Global Head of Financial Planning and Analysis. In 2015, he was appointed Treasurer of Citigroup.

Mark E. Van Der Weide

Mark E. Van Der Weide has been the General Counsel of the Federal Reserve Board since 2017. From 2010 until 2017, he worked in the Board's Division of Supervision and Regulation, helping to coordinate the development of Federal Reserve positions on international and domestic regulatory policy. Mr. Van Der Weide was detailed to the U.S. Treasury Department during 2009-2010, where he provided assistance to the Administration in its efforts to design the financial reform legislation that ultimately became the Dodd-Frank Act. From 1998 until 2009, Mr. Van Der Weide worked in the Legal Division of the Federal Reserve Board. Prior to joining the Federal Reserve Board, he worked as an associate at Cleary, Gottlieb, Steen & Hamilton. Mr. Van Der Weide received a J.D. degree from Yale Law School in 1995 and a B.A. degree in history and philosophy from the University of Iowa in 1992.

I Resolution Issues in Europe

Elke König

Keynote: The journey to resolvability

In early 2010, Paul Calello and Wilson Ervin wrote in The Economist[1]: "*What should policymakers do when faced with the potential failure of a large bank? In 2008 officials had to choose between taxpayer bail-outs (bad) or systemic financial collapse (probably worse). Various ideas to make finance safer, like contingent capital and living wills, are circulating today. But the central issue of bank resolution, perhaps the most vexing aspect of the financial crisis, has not been clearly addressed.*"

Eight years on, it is fair to say that the journey to making banks resolvable is well under way. At the international level, the G20 granted the Financial Stability Board (FSB) the mandate to steer the reform process. This effort culminated in 2011 with a framework[2] setting out the core elements that the FSB considers necessary for an effective resolution regime.

The work of the FSB has served as the blueprint for the European resolution framework, consisting of the Bank Recovery and Resolution Directive (BRRD) and the Single Resolution Mechanism (SRM) Regulation, which establishes the Single Resolution Board (SRB) as the central resolution authority within the Banking Union.

The SRB has been operational as an independent European Union (EU) Agency since January 2015, and became fully operational, with a complete set of resolution powers, on 1 January 2016. Together with the National Resolution Authorities (NRAs) of participating Member States, it forms the SRM. Its mission is to ensure an orderly resolution of failing banks with minimum impact on the real economy, the financial system, and the public finances of the participating Member States. The role of the SRB is proactive: rather than waiting for resolution cases to handle, the SRB focuses on resolution planning and preparation, with a forward-looking perspective to avoid the potential negative impact of a bank failure on the economy and on financial stability, and most of all to protect the European taxpayer.

It is worth underlining, however, that resolution is a specific procedure, introduced as an alternative to national insolvency regimes, and which under the

1 Paul Calello & Wilson Ervin, *From bail-out to bail-in*, THE ECONOMIST, January 28, 2010, available at: https://www.economist.com/node/15392186/all-comments
2 Key Attributes of Effective Resolution Regimes for Financial Institutions.

Elke König, Chair Single Resolution Board

https://doi.org/10.1515/9783110644067-001

EU regulatory framework would only apply where resolving the failing bank is in the public interest – be it out of financial stability concerns or because of the critical functions performed by the bank in the Member State.

In this context, the SRB's goal amounts to a paradigm shift seeking to end the notion that banks are "too big to fail" by ensuring that all institutions under its remit are resolvable.

Making banks resolvable

One of the key starting points to making banks resolvable is to ensure that ailing banks have sufficient funds to absorb losses and recapitalise the entity internally, thereby replacing the need for a taxpayer-funded bail-out with a privately financed "bail-in".

At EU level, the BRRD introduced the Minimum Requirement for Own Funds and Eligible Liabilities (MREL). MREL should ensure there is sufficient loss-absorption capacity by shareholders and creditors at all times to enable an effective bail-in and an orderly resolution in case a bank fails. MREL is set by the resolution authority and forms a key part of the resolution plan.

The SRB has taken a gradual, multi-year approach to MREL that takes into account the specificities of the banks under its remit, with the goal of maintaining proportionality in the system while preserving a level playing field and upholding high resolution standards across the Banking Union.

The initial approach has been to set informative MREL targets, to allow banks to prepare for their future MREL requirements. In 2017, the SRB started to address both the quantity and quality of MREL with binding requirements and bank-specific features. In the ongoing and future resolution planning cycles, we will broaden the scope to develop binding MREL targets for all major groups and also for significant entities within the groups. Building internal loss-absorbing capacity is crucial to ensure that, within a group, losses are passed from the entities where they originate to those entities where resolution action is coordinated.

MREL is a key tool to achieve resolvability, but cannot be put in place overnight. It is important for the resolution authority to retain a certain level of flexibility and realism about the capacity of particular banks to meet MREL requirements immediately. Our goal, however, is clear, and each bank must arrive at a situation where it is able to absorb losses and restore its capital position, allowing the continued performance of its critical economic functions during and after a crisis. This will call for further refinements – in quantity and quality – in the continued development of the SRB's MREL policy. Banks should be aware that MREL is here to stay, and that future requirements – in particular with regards to the quality of MREL – will increase rather than decrease.

Impediments to resolution

Resolvability, however, is not limited to MREL: it should be understood as a broader concept that embraces the manifold aspects of a bank's operations. Sufficiently high MREL levels alone cannot underpin a successful resolution if, for example, access to financial market infrastructures (FMIs) cannot be guaranteed. Indeed, a crucial task of the SRB's resolution planning involves identifying for each bank possible impediments to resolution and ensuring these are adequately addressed.

The findings from our first resolution planning cycles have revealed the following areas, among others, as potential obstacles to resolution: (i) management information systems; (ii) operational continuity; (iii) funding in resolution and (iv) group structures.

Inadequate management information systems can result in a lack of timely information essential for resolution planning and execution, or for valuation purposes. Developing the technological and operational capability to provide relevant information to resolution authorities and for supporting the implementation of resolution measures is therefore a key challenge for banks. While this may entail some investment expenditures and may impact existing systems, these costs should be weighed against the benefits in terms of supporting the day-to-day management, increased transparency and enabling a coherent management, both in business as usual and in resolution.

Secondly, ensuring operational continuity in resolution and maintaining access to financial market infrastructures and FMI intermediaries ahead of, and during resolution is another important element of ensuring resolvability. This requires, among others, banks to identify and map all services necessary for the provision of critical functions and critical business lines; setting up a repository of all service level agreements and contracts with critical internal and external service providers, which should be resolution-proof; and identifying and mapping all critical FMI services from FMIs and FMI intermediaries.

Furthermore, financial arrangements must be in place to ensure that during and after resolution access to liquidity and funding is maintained or regained to safeguard the continuation of the bank's critical functions, regardless of whether they will remain within the bank under resolution or will be transferred to a third party purchaser or to a bridge bank. In the period leading up to the failure of the bank, it is likely that liquidity needs have increased, funding has become more expensive and collateral requirements have increased.

Finally, banks, particularly large cross-border ones, are characterized by complex group structures which can present a barrier to their resolvability. A resolution authority must therefore ensure that the legal and funding structures of the group facilitate the implementation of the preferred resolution strategy. This implies identifying and removing sources of undue complexity in the legal structure, as well as developing plans for achieving a sufficient amount of appropriate loss-absorbing instruments in the right location.

Building resolvability together

Building resolvability is not a task for the regulator alone. The SRB relies on the good cooperation and compliance of the industry: the SRB will set the focus and provide the impulse, but banks themselves are expected to make changes in their organisational structure and operations to facilitate their orderly resolution in case of crisis. The SRB will subsequently monitor and assess the progress made in achieving banks' resolvability.

The banks are well aware of the different aspects that should be addressed to make themselves resolvable and should therefore proceed without waiting for detailed regulators' instructions. Responsible bank management teams will already be working on these areas, and we encourage those lagging behind to follow the lead of others in the industry. Given the favourable economic climate, now is the time to address such issues.

Moreover, the SRB cooperates with the national competent authorities. This close relationship with authorities who have their finger on the pulse locally is essential to our work, as it allows us to address the specific issues related to particular banks and to adequately reflect national specificities.

Completing the jigsaw

Making banks more resolvable also requires strengthening the regulatory framework and finalising the institutional architecture.

The revision of the BRRD, with the transposition of the international total loss absorbing capacity (TLAC) standard in EU legislation, is a key milestone towards finalising the rules under which the SRB operates and providing clarity to the industry and investors, particularly on MREL. Complexity should be avoided where possible; transparency and predictability are of utmost importance for the institutions and for the markets. Yet, it is important that the SRB retain discretion and flexibility for the purpose of MREL setting and calibration, to ensure a level playing field for credit institutions in the Banking Union.

More broadly, completing the Banking Union must be a priority for the European Union in the months ahead. This entails setting up a common backstop to the single resolution fund (SRF) and establishing a European Deposit Insurance Scheme, as the third pillar of the Banking Union.

A well-designed backstop, available as a last resort, will give markets the confidence that large, complex banks are truly resolvable, and reduce stress on the financial system in the event of a bank failure.

A backstop, however, will not solve by itself the key issue of funding in resolution, which needs to be addressed jointly with other authorities. While the resolution framework provides for powers and tools to restore the solvency of failing institutions, even if the bank is well recapitalised after the resolution week-end, it is expected that it will still experience liquidity stress as market confidence might take some time to reappear.

The SRF can contribute to the provision of funding in resolution. However, considering its capacity, articulation with other sources of funding is required to handle the failure of a large complex bank or a series of banks. Cooperation and a common understanding with central banks to address gaps in the current framework will be of vital importance to make progress. Developing an effective solution would give market participants the confidence to provide funding to banks soon after the resolution weekend, and in turn may limit the need to access such facilities.

Finally, we are currently faced with 19 different insolvency regimes in the Banking Union alone. This makes the analysis of the insolvency counterfactual for a cross-border bank in resolution highly challenging, and results in diverging outcomes depending on the home country of the institution. Bank insolvency procedures should be elevated to a common best standard and practice at EU level. The ideal solution would be EU wide rules on insolvency proceedings for the banking sector, with the development of national handbooks by the resolution authorities as just a 'second best' option.

Conclusion

At the peak of the crisis, large banks were considered too big, too complex and too interconnected to fail, raising a moral hazard issue as bail-outs were chosen for lack of a better alternative.

The regulatory response has determined a fundamental paradigm shift, and bail-in rather than bail-out is now the norm. According to a simulation by the European Commission, the benefits to the real economy of higher bank capital requirements introduced under CRD IV and the new bail-in rules deliver combined macroeconomic benefits amounting to 0.6%-1.1% of EU GDP per year, while the macroeconomic costs of these reforms amount to a mere 0.3% of GDP.

Some are arguing that the regulatory tightening which occurred in the wake of the crisis has been excessive and that a loosening of the screws is now warranted. On the contrary, we maintain that regulatory backsliding, when many new rules are still panning out, would be a mistake. Given the current favourable economic climate, now is rather the time to continue implementing the post-crisis rules to make sure the system is better prepared against future shocks.

The regulations that have been adopted since the crisis, and the technical work undertaken on resolution, mean that many banks can now safely enter insolvency without causing disruption to financial stability. The work to make banks resolvable, however, is not over. As we are keen on saying, resolution is a process, not a product. The combined efforts of the regulators and the industry to refine resolution plans and address impediments to resolvability must go on.

Andreas Dombret

A brief progress report on the resolution framework in Europe

Introduction

One of the key lessons of the financial crisis was understanding the dangers of banks that are "too big to fail" and their costs to the taxpayer in terms of public bailouts. In Europe, legislative responses to this included the adoption of a new European resolution framework and the introduction of a European resolution authority, thus transposing into European law the FSB Key Attributes of Effective Resolution Regimes for Financial Institutions. Today, with the European resolution framework now fully implemented and in force, a crucial question arises: does the new resolution regime fulfil its initial objectives? Recent events have led some to doubt the general approach of the new regime. This article argues that instead of questioning the general direction of the resolution framework, analyses have to carefully distinguish between different cases and identify specific impediments to the regime. Also, it has to be acknowledged that even though the legal framework has been established, the sector is still in the process of transitioning to the new resolution regime.

Background

In order to properly assess the new resolution regime in Europe, we need to recall how things were prior to its introduction. In the grand scheme of things, the flaws in the former regulatory framework can be summarised as major inconsistencies in a market economy. There were banks that were too big to fail and some were bailed out by governments, showing that the path of least resistance was to use taxpayers' money to stabilise the financial system. Indeed, under the conditions at the time, this may have been the only tenable course of action at all. For managers and investors, this worsened existing bad incentives such as "gambling for resurrection" – which means focusing on the unlikely prospects of recovery.

Andreas Dombret, Member of the Board of Deutsche Bundesbank (May 2010-May 2018)
Member of the Board of the Bank for International Settlements

https://doi.org/10.1515/9783110644067-002

As a consequence, and on top of an overhaul of capital and liquidity regulation, the "new" resolution regime for banks was developed to overcome these market economy inconsistencies. Restoring the principles of the market economy provided a solution to the political dilemma of having to decide between systemically risky insolvency proceedings on the one hand, and economically and politically questionable bail-outs on the other.

To overcome this, the basic idea is that if an institution fails, its shareholders and creditors should be the first in line to take on the risks and absorb the losses. While the actual realisation of a credible resolution regime is a lot more complex, the underlying idea should still serve as the yardstick for evaluating resolutions in Europe going forward.

Assessing how the new regime has dealt with distressed banks thus far

All the components of the new architecture are now in place and we now also have some first-hand empirical evidence of how it works in practice, due to events involving ailing institutions in Spain and Italy.

There is an important overall point to make right at the outset, which is that we have not seen lasting spillover effects or negative repercussions in the markets in the Spanish or the Italian cases. The resolution of Banco Popular Español, in particular, shows that despite the doubts of many experts in the wake of the financial crisis, the overnight resolution of a large European bank is possible. Indeed, the resolution of Banco Popular Español went largely unnoticed by financial markets and the wider public.

But of course, proof that the new regime can work properly *in principle* does not settle further debates. Moreover, over the past year we have witnessed several weaknesses in the existing set of rules (concerning past bank failures). At some point in the future, when the European Commission reviews the Bank Recovery and Resolution Directive (as foreseen in the Directive), the lessons learned so far will need to be taken into account and the legislation amended accordingly.

A key concern in this respect is that one of the major objectives of the European resolution regime, i.e. to shield the (national) taxpayer from risks entered into by owners and investors, needs to be applied in a consistent manner in all cases of ailing banks, i.e. those which involve resolution actions and those that do not. In essence, the spirit of the main objective of the "new" EU resolution framework, i.e. for shareholders and creditors to bear losses instead of taxpayers, should be preserved even when banks that are liquidated according to national insolvency regimes require state aid to facilitate their liquidation or their market exit.

Where the resolution authority decides that resolution action is not in the public interest, the resulting shift from the resolution regime to a national insolvency regime must not be allowed to create a whole new ball game. Instead, the same underlying principle of protecting the taxpayer should remain paramount, even if there is no resolution in a narrower sense.

In the event that state aid is required to facilitate the liquidation of an ailing bank, European state aid rules apply, including those pursuant to the 2013 Banking Communication. These require, as a rule, that shareholders and subordinated debt fully contribute before state aid can be granted (so-called burden-sharing). Thus, there is a significant difference when it comes to the protection of taxpayers, depending on whether the resolution framework or the national insolvency rules apply. This could lead to wrong incentives and might also fail to meet the resolution framework's declared aim of protecting taxpayers' money.

In order to ensure that national taxpayers are adequately protected, irrespective of whether resolution action is taken or not, it is therefore essential that European state aid rules are aligned with European resolution rules.

One solution could be to amend the 2013 Banking Communication by extending the burden-sharing requirements analogous to the Bank Recovery and Resolution Directive (minimum of 8% total liabilities) for cases in which the bank is to be liquidated according to national insolvency rules (where it is deemed that a resolution is not in the public interest). Considering that the Banking Communication has not been reviewed or updated since its entry into force (which was in 2013 and therefore prior to the European resolution regime coming into force), a general revision in order to align the content to the EU law in force today seems appropriate.

But reforms not only need to respond to actual cases in which institutions are failing or likely to fail, they also need to adjust to other potential weaknesses. One of these potential weaknesses can be found in the current legal construction of a precautionary recapitalisation tool. When it was introduced in the resolution framework, it was designated for rare and very exceptional cases only. Accordingly, a precautionary recapitalisation is, by law, only permissible under certain conditions. For example, the institution must be deemed solvent, and the public funds may not be used to offset existing or anticipated losses. Supervisors need to carefully examine whether these requirements are met. Additionally, the European Commission has to decide whether the granting of public funds by way of a precautionary recapitalisation is compatible with EU state aid rules. Restricting the applicability of this policy tool happened for good reasons and therefore precautionary recapitalisation must not be seen as a blueprint for averting bank crises. This is because one of the fundamental objectives of the "new" resolution framework is to shield taxpayers. It should be a bank's shareholders and creditors who are on the hook for unsatisfactory bank management and any losses that arise as a result, not taxpayers.

However, the application criteria still lack clarity. As a consequence, an extensive use of this instrument, which was intended as an exception to the rule, cannot be ruled out. A redrafting of the text by adding more clarity and detail to the criteria could therefore be very useful, considering that its first application last year already revealed some inaccuracies and vagueness of this provision – likely due to the fact that it was added very late in the drafting process of the BRRD.

Continuing the transition into the era of resolution

With the need to further strengthen the regulatory framework in the future, an evaluation of our European resolution regime also needs to take into account the overall timeline of the project. The full transition from the old to the new regime requires not only the new rules that have come into force, but also a transition with new responsibilities, new roles for investors, and a new role for society. It was clear at the outset that some of these changes would not take place painlessly. Furthermore, although the "new" regime has now been implemented in all member states, it is still a "young" framework and we are still in the operationalising phase. This applies with regard to recovery and resolution planning, removal of barriers to resolvability, and the application of early intervention powers. We have to further improve the practical implementation of the rules foreseen in the framework, particularly by avoiding undue delays in any future "failing or likely to fail" assessments, since such delays imply increasing costs and render resolution or liquidation more difficult in the end. Furthermore, once in resolution, a firm application of the bail-in tool is essential to ensure that taxpayers are not held liable for the costs of bank failures.

But banks have to play their part in the transition, too. A major aspect relates to bail-inable capital. I am aware that this requirement will not be achieved overnight and needs some time, but unnecessary delays must be avoided. Accordingly, banks are starting to build up their bail-inable loss absorbing capacity (TLAC/MREL). In order for this capacity to be both credible and usable when required, institutions will have to build up a sufficient amount. To achieve this aim, it is very important that any suggestions which could weaken the requirements for MREL should be seriously reconsidered in the course of the ongoing review of the EU legal framework.

Conclusion

At the height of the financial crisis, some thought it would be impossible to transition to a new resolution regime. It is therefore all the more remarkable that none of the first resolution cases led to lasting spillover effects or negative repercussions in the markets. This demonstrates that, in principle, markets trust Europe's "new" resolution regime to allow for an orderly resolution of distressed banks. It should also encourage us to further strengthen our efforts to rigorously address existing loopholes.

But also, as a general rule, every crisis tends to be different and there is no "one size fits all" approach to resolving them. We observed this recently in Italy and Spain. The institutions differed in terms of the reasons why they ran into difficulties, their positions in the banking market and their standing in their respective economies. So we have also learned that we can only speak of success if all components of the new regime work properly and are credible. Even "small" loopholes could be enough to allow the fragilities of the old regime to persist.

Furthermore, the main task of establishing a regime for banks that is compatible with the market economy goes beyond specific resolution issues. We also have to find answers for ongoing challenges such as the sovereign bank nexus, which must be resolved to prevent a sovereign debt crisis leading to a financial sector crisis and vice versa. For financial stability, reducing concentration risk and backing sovereign debt exposure with adequate regulatory risk capital is essential.

Adam Farkas

Resolution in Europe, still some way to go

Resolution "train-spotters" like to comment that the European Union (EU) is lagging behind its peers in terms of implementing the globally agreed resolution framework. This might be true to some extent, the EU started somewhat behind, but has made a lot of progress.

Resolution represents a radical shift in the way European authorities deal with bank failures – moving from a setting primarily based on bail-out by public funds to relying on the bail-in of private claims. This means changing the legal framework and imposing significant change on the way banks are structured and operate. Executing change of such magnitude takes time and understandably, today, a number of issues remain outstanding.

The European Union was (and still is) highly banked...

Banks differ from other businesses in that they cannot necessarily be left to fail under normal insolvency procedures. This is because they provide services which can be critical to an economy. Banks were (and still are) particularly critical to the European economy – as was evidenced in the crisis.

In 2012, bank loans represented 250% of the EU's GDP against 60% in the US. Over the years, this large banking sector has gone through waves of consolidation, which have resulted in a high proportion of large and complex banks.

Note: I would like to thank my colleagues Spiridon Zarkos and Thibault Godbillon for their invaluable assistance in preparing this article. Any views expressed are solely my own and so cannot be taken to represent those of the European Banking Authority (EBA) or to state EBA policy. Neither the EBA nor any person acting on behalf may be held responsible for the use which may be made of the information contained in this publication, or for any errors which, despite careful preparation and checking, may appear.

Adam Farkas, Executive Director, European Banking Authority

https://doi.org/10.1515/9783110644067-003

For instance, as of November 2017 the EU was home to 13 of the 30 most complex banks in the world as determined by the Financial Stability Board (FSB).[1] In addition to these 13 globally systemic banks, the European supervisory authorities have identified another circa 120 other systemically important institutions (O-SIIs), domestic banking groups or stand-alone banks which are considered systemic from a local point of view. With an additional dozen subsidiaries of third country banks, which are all considered as locally systemically important.

The population of banks is then complemented by around another 2800 smaller banking groups and stand-alone banks considered as less significant.

...and it had no framework to deal with banking crisis

Ten years ago, when the crisis hit Europe, neither individual member states in the EU, nor the EU as a whole, had the necessary regime to deal with bank failures. EU member states did not have adequate deposit guarantee schemes to prevent bank runs on cross border banks, and there was no authority in charge of managing failing banks equipped with the necessary powers to intervene, e.g. powers to impose losses on creditors, take over a bank, remove management or force a sale.

At the EU level, cooperation arrangements for crisis management were not up to the task. The EBA's predecessor, the committee of European Banking Supervisors (CEBS), was the only European banking regulatory organisation with a cross-border view, and it had no effective powers over banks. As a result, when cross border groups started failing, national interest took precedent and cross border cooperation did not work.

Finally, the systemic aspect of the crisis meant that the usual recipe of arranging a marriage between a failing bank and a stronger one was not widely available as a solution. It was tried, and while some marriages worked many didn't, with the acquisition either not going through or contributing to the failure of the acquirer.

Ultimately, European taxpayers ended-up having to pay to recapitalise these failing banks to ensure they would continue to provide critical services without bringing down other banks with them. The cost of these bailouts was particularly high in countries such as Greece and Ireland where it reached more

---

1 FSB – 2017 list of global systemically important banks (G-SIBs), November 2017 and down from 15 back in 2011 when the list was first established.

than 30% of the GDP. But also, in Germany, the UK or the Netherlands where the cost averaged 15% of GDP, and 10% in Spain.

The sheer size of losses was beyond many countries' fiscal capacity, and triggered sovereign debt stress and further market disruption in 2011/12.

The EU now has a strong harmonized framework

Immediately after the crisis, the EU and member states, which were home or host to global systemically important banks (G-SIBs), have played a leading role in shaping the global supervisory and resolution framework via their involvement in the newly expanded G20 and FSB.

Following international agreement on the key attributes of effective resolution regimes in October 2011, the European Union adopted in 2014 a harmonised crisis management framework – the Bank Recovery and Resolution Directive (BRRD) – which came into force in 2015. The new directive, which has been transposed into national law in all EU member states, introduced harmonized powers allowing every EU member state to be in a position to intervene in case of a bank failure.

BRRD has introduced clear resolution objectives for all resolution authorities in the EU: (i) ensure continuity of critical functions, (ii) avoid adverse effects on financial stability, (iii) protect public funds, (iv) protect depositors and (v) protect clients' funds and assets and the while minimizing the cost of resolution.

To meet these objectives, BRRD has ensured that in all 28 member states an independent authority was established with the powers[2] to:

- Access information to prepare resolution actions,
- Taking control of a bank under resolution, including the power to replace the management,
- Exercising rights and powers conferred upon shareholders and the management body,
- Transferring shares, rights, assets or liabilities,
- Altering the maturity of eligible liabilities, converting them into shares or reducing the principal amount, and
- Cancelling or reducing the nominal amount of shares or other instruments of ownership.

2 Directive 2014/59/EU (BRRD) 63–72.

In addition to setting out the powers necessary to deal with a bank failure, BRRD also sets out how resolution planning is to be carried out. Resolution authorities have been tasked with the responsibility to plan for banking failure i.e. agree resolution strategies for specific banks, preparing resolution plans, and enforce the necessary changes on these banks to ensure the credibility of the strategy.

BRRD has also improved the early intervention framework for supervisory authorities and formalized the requirement for banks to draw recovery plans – good practice until then, but now a requirement which ensures that banks have easily executable and capital generating options in times of stress.

Finally, BRRD has also introduced a clear framework to deal with cross border resolution with the concept of resolution colleges. Resolution colleges are fora for ongoing interactive engagement between the participants in order to plan and execute the effective resolution of cross-border banking groups. The resolution colleges' role is wider and more significant than the simple process of holding physical meetings or conference calls.

To deal with the insufficient cross border cooperation in bank supervision in the EU, the EBA was first created with the aim to upgrade the quality and consistency of national supervision, strengthening oversight of cross-border groups and establishing a European single rule book applicable to all financial institutions in the internal market.

Deeper integration was then achieved in 2013 within the Eurozone, but also opening the door to non-Eurozone EU members with the creation of the Single Supervisory Mechanism (SSM) and the Single Resolution Board (SRB).

As a credit to the importance of the change in the framework, shortly after BRRD came into force, rating agencies started removing sovereign support from their ratings for European banks, effectively signalling the reduction of moral hazard stemming from the implicit support provided by the anticipation of public bail-out of banks.

Since the crisis the resolvability of the largest banks has improved

From 2015 onwards, equipped with these new powers, resolution authorities across the EU have been put to work. 2018 saw the start of the third resolution planning cycle and so far significant progress has been achieved – in particular with respect to the largest firms.

Resolution strategies: Resolution strategies have been agreed and plans have been drafted for all globally and other -systemic important institutions (G/O-SIIs) in the EU. The plans set-out in writing a strategy agreed between the key authorities involved -the resolution authority(ies) and the supervisory authority(ies).

Resolution colleges have been established for all cross-border groups in the EU. This is a key piece of the puzzle where all relevant authorities have now in place a forum to share information, take decisions and coordinate action.

MREL/TLAC for G-SIIs: There has been strong issuance of total loss absorbing capital (TLAC) eligible debt during 2017/2018, and the introduction of the senior non-preferred class in some member states has been welcomed. Almost all European G-SIIs are meeting the first TLAC minimum applying from January 2019. All EU G-SIIs have been set minimum requirements for own funds and eligible liabilities (MREL) far in excess of TLAC minimum requirements – close to twice minimum capital requirements to be met by January 2022 – in line with TLAC.

MREL for O-SIIs: Outside of the Banking Union, most domestic O-SIIs have been set MREL targets to be met by 2023 at the latest – with full subordination requirements. Within the Banking Union, the SRB has prioritized the largest cross-border groups for which it has set MREL requirements, again broadly at twice capital requirement, and expected to do so for the others by end 2019.

Stays on financial contracts: Some EU G-SIIs have made significant progress with regards to close out risks of financial contracts with exposures fully covered by either International Swaps and Derivatives Association (ISDA) protocols or contractual recognition of stay powers.

BRRD has forced banks to generate information and provide it to authorities – information generally not available before:

a) **Liability structure**: as banks build up their loss absorbing capacity, authorities have improved their understanding of its structure, the instruments which would be available in crisis, their contractual features, instruments which would create issues, etc.
b) **Critical economic functions**: in an exchange with banks, authorities have identified functions, which are seen as critical and must be maintained as a priority in resolution. This is key to inform the choice of strategy and support effective planning.
c) **Operational continuity**: one of the objectives of resolution is to maintain continuity of services, which requires the identification of which function rely on which services a bank operates. Banks have started working on

identifying these services and corresponding contracts and organizing them in central repositories making them easily accessible.

d) **Access to FMIs**: to continue to operate, banks need to maintain access to financial market infrastructures. The first step was to improve the understanding of both banks and authorities of the interconnectedness generated by the provision of access to FMIs. This is now done for most banks.
e) **Funding in resolution**: both banks and authorities have improved their understanding of banks' funding and liquidity needs in resolution, the location and availability of collateral.
f) **Solvent wind down**: some authorities in the EU, host to third country G-SIIs with investment bank activities, have had banks carry out exercises to assess the costs of winding down large trading books.

But resolution authorities have to set MREL and banks need to build up credible loss absorbing capacity (LAC)

Effective loss absorbing capacity is the key to successful resolution – for bail-in or other strategies (bridge bank, transfer). Without LAC, resolution authorities have little room for maneuver in resolution – unless maybe to rely on a healthy buyer with deep pockets, ready to quickly acquire a failing bank. Still then, the resolution authority could generate moral hazard by fully compensating senior creditors while potentially putting another bank at risk. The EBA, as part of its work program, will be contributing to monitoring the implementation of MREL and the build-up of LAC in the EU.

MREL for Banking Union O-SIIs: Not all O-SIIs in the EU have been set MREL. As of June 2018, about two thirds of European O-SIIs have not been formally communicated a set MREL target. These banks have engaged with their resolution authority, are aware that the requirement is coming and are expected to issue instruments to meet the target. But until resolution authorities set a clear MREL target there is a reduced likelihood that banks will issue as required.

Subordination: Another area where MREL differs from TLAC is that it is up to the relevant resolution authority to decide on the adequate level of subordination for the effective implementation of the resolution strategy. One of the safeguards of the European resolution framework is the no creditor worse off principle (NCWO).[3] In a resolution, any creditor which ends-up worse than he would have been in insolvency is entitled to compensation – this equates to partially bailing out these creditor – potentially with public money. The key to deal with NCWO risk is to require a clear subordination of creditors who are expected to absorb losses in resolution. This has the advantage of creating a class of instruments clearly bail-inable – easily identifiable by both investors and regulators. This facilitates the imposition of losses on creditors.

At present, in the EU, banks for which an MREL decision has been made represent circa EUR 7.2 trillion in risk weighted assets, but 70% of those do not have a clear subordination requirements. This does not prevent resolution authorities from bailing-in some creditors, but it won't be easy and some creditors may need to be compensated, potentially with public money in case the NCWO principle is not deemed to have been applied.

Internal MREL for third country banks: The mechanism by which losses are passed from subsidiaries to the resolution entity has not been agreed. This is particularly key for EU based subsidiaries of third country banks. The EU is host to subsidiaries of all third country G-SIIs and until, adequate internal loss absorbing capacity is being down-streamed in these entities, which are deemed material – the European banking sector remains vulnerable.

Internal MREL within EU groups: It is essential for home and host authorities to agree on how the externally issued LAC is distributed within the group. Within the European framework as set out by BRRD, this requires reaching binding joint decisions within resolution colleges. This needs to be agreed in a manner which works for both home and host authorities. On the one hand, home authorities need to respect host authorities' assessment of criticality of subsidiaries, and provide necessary support agreements. But at the same time host resolution authorities need to trust banking groups to support their subsidiaries in crisis, in particular if those are relatively small within the group.

Both banks and authorities still have a lot to do to allow the orderly resolution of banks

Building up adequate loss absorbing capacity is probably more than half the job – in particular if the resolution strategy is bail-in. But, to ensure that a bank

---

3 Directive 2014/59/EU (BRRD) Art. 74.

can actually maintain all critical services from day one and that the resolved bank can effectively continue to operate smoothly on Monday morning – there is a lot more resolution authorities need to do.

As prescribed by BRRD, resolution authorities have made major efforts drafting plans summarizing the information received. Progress in actually changing banks' structure and making them more resolvable has been slow. We are in the third resolution planning cycle and all authorities and banks are working on improving resolvability, and some authorities have made more progress than others. But European banks who have actually completed all the keys steps described below are the exception rather than the rule.

Operational continuity[4]: Banks have identified their key contracts and started building repositories to make contracts readily available on short notice. But this isn't enough to ensure continuity, banks need to ensure that contracts are effectively resolution proof, that financial resources are secured, that a proper governance is in place, that key people are retained and that rights to access/use operational assets by the service provider are clear. This is something that can potentially be dealt with in contingency for small and simple firms but not for large cross-border banking groups.

Access to FMIs[5]: Most banks have identified their key FMIs, and who they provide access to, but few have actually reached out to FMIs to agree on the steps to take in resolution or sized the liquidity needs to maintain access or carried out an impact assessment of the loss of a critical FMI. Resolution authorities in conjunction with FMI supervisors need to agree on contingency plans in case of resolution.

Bail-in execution[6]: All resolution authorities in the EU are one way or another working on this issue, and some are more advanced than others but none have actually solved all the key questions. For instance, the FSB guidelines on bail-in execution list the following areas, which need to be addressed: (i) bail-in scope, (ii) valuation, (iii) exchange mechanics, (iv) securities laws and exchange requirements, (v) resolution governance, (vi) resolution communications. As part of its work program, the EBA will contribute to develop a harmonised approach to resolution execution focusing on valuation and securities law and exchange requirements.

---

4 FSB Guidance on Arrangements to Support Operational Continuity in Resolution, August 2016.

5 FSB Guidance on Continuity of Access to Financial Market Infrastructures for a Firm in Resolution, July 2017.

6 FSB Principles on Bail-in Execution, June 2018.

Funding and liquidity: As mentioned in the previous sections, both banks and authorities have made progress in understanding their funding needs in resolution, but they still need to ensure that there are operational arrangement effectively in place, which would allow liquidity to be provided. For instance, few countries have clearly set-up how and under which terms a resolved bank could access temporary public sector backstop facilities. Authorities of different countries/ currencies need to allocate responsibilities and clearly set out the sequencing on funding and communication to the market. Finally, authorities still have work to do on ensuring that they have the right indicators to assess liquidity stress in resolution, and that the resolution funding plan is coherent with the recovery/contingency funding arrangements.[7]

Disclosure / transparency: There is a need to increase transparency to ensure the framework is understood. This is particularly true in the context of bail-in, and will be partly addressed as part of revised Pillar 3 disclosure for G-SIIs. But an adequate framework needs to be introduced for all banks and needs to go beyond LAC.

Recovery and resolution: Recovery and resolution plans lack consistency to ensure a smooth continuum in crisis management. For instance, critical functions are not necessarily aligned, funding plans are not credibly linked, the impact of recovery actions on resolvability isn't assessed. But more generally coordination between authorities in both the planning phase and run-up to resolution tends to be below the optimal level. The EBA as part of its work program will be working with both resolution and supervisory authorities the consistency between recovery and resolution plans and the overall continuum between recovery and resolution.

Resolution colleges: Colleges need to maintain an active dialogue and to progress in ensuring involvement of all parties to become more operational. All members need to contribute effectively focusing on progress on resolvability, ensuring financial stability for all hosts and ensuring effective arrangement via simulation exercises. The EBA will continue to monitor the good functioning of resolution colleges after it published its first report on their progress in July 2017.[8]

Finally, it has become clear to resolution authorities and to legislators that insolvency regimes are different in different EU members. While BRRD has introduced a consistent resolution framework, liquidation remains fragmented. This creates issues in the context of resolution planning. Resolution cases in 2017

---

7 FSB Funding Strategy Elements of an Implementable Resolution Plan, June 2018.
8 EBA report on the functioning of resolution colleges in 2017, July 2018.

illustrated how liquidation can lead to public funds being used in the context of winding-down a bank. But diverging insolvency laws also create significant issues when assessing the no creditor worse off risk.

For the smaller banks the situation and the progress are less clear

In most European member states, resolution authorities prioritised the largest cross-border banks in their effort. This is understandable considering that the largest banks are the most likely to threaten financial stability and to potentially require public funds if bail out remains the only option.

But within today's framework all banks are now expected to either go into resolution or liquidation in case of failure – with a preference for liquidation for the 2800 smaller banks. So, it is important for authorities to establish their risk appetite for using the national insolvency procedure.

The impact of the failure of a small regional bank can appear limited and unlikely to trigger a domino effect on other banks. But, even a small bank holds retail deposits, even a small bank holds SME deposits. Losing access to these funds could have very direct effect on individuals or SMEs even if only for 7 days[9]

What the EBA has found is that as of June 2018 only four resolution authorities had set both strategies and MREL for all their domestic LSIs – the rest has either only set the strategy or done neither.

Firstly, without clarity on which strategy would be applied in case of resolution, banks cannot progress on making themselves resolvable or ready to facilitate a deposit payout in insolvency. The less complex the bank is, the easier it is to deal with the technicalities of resolution in contingency planning. This would still require excellent coordination between the supervisory and resolution authorities to allow sufficient time to prepare, which isn't yet the case in some jurisdictions.

Second, without clear MREL targets, banks cannot reasonably plan their funding needs and, again, resolution without MREL isn't credible. And raising MREL for smaller banks might not be easy – some might not have access to wholesale markets. A resolution strategy requiring additional MREL for a bank which cannot raise it implies significant changes – either de-risking and exit of certain activities or considering M&A to gain a critical mass.

9 Directive 2014/49/EU (DGSD) Art. 8.1.

Why isn't the European Union more advanced – what needs to be amended in the framework?

BRRD is currently being reviewed so as to facilitate the implementation of TLAC and internal MREL. A more comprehensive review is expected later, and this will provide the opportunity to address a number of issues which have become clear during the implementation of the framework. Some of the most important ones for consideration are set out below.

Structural separation between supervision and resolution. BRRD has introduced the independence of resolution authorities so as to prevent supervisory forbearance in the run-up to resolution/liquidation. But an overly strict reading of BRRD has led to difficulties in relation to access to information or involvement in decisions making in contingency planning, which have prevented some resolution authorities from effectively planning ahead for their resolution week-end. Information sharing needs to be improved and the place of the resolution authorities in the supervisory decision making process should be clarified.

Make resolvability a supervisory objective. More generally, there is a need for resolvability to become a clear supervisory objective – banks need to be supervised so as to be resolvable. Improved resolvability is in the interest of supervisors as a bank is more likely to stay out of resolution if it is resolvable – creditors will chose restructuring outside of resolution rather than within – at least they'll have a say on the terms. For instance, resolvability could feed into the SREP process.

The responsibility for resolution planning. BRRD made the choice of putting the responsibility of resolution planning into the hands of the authorities – under the principle that those who would be in charge of executing resolution should be holding the pen. This is supported by the notion that authorities have a better view of what is beneficial for the economy in a crisis beyond the interests of shareholders and creditors. But it must acknowledged that there should be a greater involvement of banks in the process. Some authorities have experienced or are considering a self-assessment process, so as to ensure better ownership of resolvability by the banks. Once the objectives of the resolution strategy are agreed, banks are much better positioned to best meet these objectives due to their intimate knowledge of their own organization. This would leave time for the authorities to review and push banks on making progress instead of compiling data to make plans as a compliance exercise.

Discrepancies in the liquidation regimes. There is a clear need for aligning liquidation regimes, resolution triggers and state-aid rules so as to avoid public money being used in insolvency to support the liquidation of a failed bank and to facilitate NCWO compensation.

Conclusion

Implementing the globally agreed bank resolution framework in Europe is work in progress. Within the framework provided by BRRD, authorities across the Union are equipped to deal with bank failures. But to ensure the orderly resolution of failing banks, banks and authorities still have a lot of work to do.

Loss absorbing capacity is the cornerstone of resolution under all strategies, and needs to be clear for banks, authorities and investors. Quantum, location and quality need to be further specified for all banks.

Resolvability needs to improve. Authorities need to specify their expectations, do their part in bail-in execution, access to FMIs or liquidity while banks need to effectively progress in making themselves resolvable – with supervisory authorities fully supporting these efforts.

Coordination between supervisory and resolution authorities needs to improve. Information needs to be shared immediately, resolution authorities need to be consulted in all decisions in contingency planning and in the run-up to resolution.

The future BRRD review will be the opportunity to update the framework and address some of these key outstanding issues.

James von Moltke

Practice and international comparison of resolution regimes

Introduction

The 2008 financial crisis demonstrated that banks needed to adapt to ensure that their failure could no longer impact the financial sector with consequences for the wider economy. This entails ensuring that the resolution strategy is successful (i.e. by removing impediments to resolution) and where possible decreasing the overall complexity of the institution. Building market confidence in the resolution framework relies on all global, systemically-important banks ("G-SIBs") and in some cases, domestically-important banks ("D-SIBs") progressing at the same pace and level of maturity on crucial dimensions, such as operationalising bail-in, and increasing transparency on the part of both banks and regulators on this progress and prioritisation.

The resolution regulatory framework, certainly in the EU, is moving in the right direction and provides key pre-requisites for continuity post resolution, for example, a stay on terminations. However, some key topics remain unresolved such as liquidity and the role of central banks, or financial market infrastructures (FMI) continuity. While banks are trying to address them, they alone do not have the definitive answers and therefore need support from the regulatory community. Finally, continued efforts to demonstrate that the European framework is solid will further strengthen cross-border cooperation on resolution.

In this article, we will examine several questions which we see as fundamental to the success of a resolution regulatory framework: Does resolution work? Can the Bank Recovery and Resolution Directive (BRRD) work given the differences between the insolvency laws of different member states? Where does the EU stand relative to the U.S.? How important is co-operation between regulatory and supervisory bodies in a resolution scenario? In each case, we will examine the factors which will be decisive in determining the answers to these questions.

James von Moltke, Chief Financial Officer of Deutsche Bank

https://doi.org/10.1515/9783110644067-004

Does resolution work?

Resolution has to work. The alternatives – for example, a major bank entering insolvency, as in the case of Lehman Brothers, or a taxpayer bail-out – are neither viable nor palatable for the stability of either the financial system or for the global economy. The following factors are critical: regulatory cooperation, operational readiness of banks; the ability of regulators to execute resolution; and the potential to limit any systemic shut-down, especially in credit markets, as a consequence of the bail-in of a large institution.

Firstly, a successful resolution event requires cooperation between the home and host authority. In any situation, but especially in a stress event, it is of the utmost importance that home supervisors and resolution authorities work in close partnership. The speed of deterioration which can be expected in a crisis, requires well established communication paths and clear understanding of roles and responsibilities. In addition, host authorities need to have confidence in the resolution plan and a solid understanding of how the plan could impact their jurisdiction. Crisis Management Groups (CMG) are proving very useful for precisely this reason, and help foster cooperation amongst home and host authorities.

Secondly, in considering ex-ante operational readiness it is crucial that G/D-SIBs demonstrate this by undertaking the necessary technical groundwork to embed capabilities within the bank. This includes being 'ready and able' to calculate and write-down bail-in-able liabilities, the capital gap at the point of resolution and having capabilities in place to execute debt to equity swaps. Business reorganisation planning is also essential to demonstrate that there is a predefined, decisive, set of strategic actions that can be taken after the bail-in event.

Lastly, the possibility of predicting the impact a G/D-SIB bail-in would have from a systemic perspective is always limited. One avenue to mitigate against the potential systemic impact of a resolution event is to communicate the business reorganisation plan to the market to demonstrate that the failed bank will be restructured in a manner which ensures ongoing viability after the resolution event. For this to be effective, banks need to identify potential post-resolution business strategies before a resolution event (this is also needed to perform the franchise valuation which ultimately informs the conversion of debt to equity).

Can the BRRD work with differences in member states' insolvency laws?

Potential problems arise from the differences between different EU member states. Whilst these problems do not render the BRRD ineffective, they do pose challenges to a successful resolution; starting with the ranking of debt in insolvency, notably for the Minimum Requirements for own Funds and Eligible Liabilities (MREL) and Total Loss Absorbing Capacity (TLAC). However, the problem goes further than that. It extends to differences in insolvency procedures and speed, rules on collateral and other problems in connection with the difficulties in implementing the Capital Markets Union (CMU).

In furthering the CMU in Europe, three considerations are key:

- Firstly, the path to a 'level playing field': the insolvency hierarchy is fragmented across Europe. Germany has opted for retrospective subordination whereas France uses contractual subordination, requiring new TLAC to be issued. It is hard to see how we can really create greater reliance on debt markets without a common insolvency hierarchy. One of the key pillars of the union is the harmonization of insolvency regimes as well as the standardization of their application. A step forward in this direction is the recently harmonized ranking of unsecured debt instruments for EU institutions.
- Secondly, transparency over bail-in risk is paramount: in the past, doubts over their position in the hierarchy caused investors to act precipitately. Whilst investors indicate that they now understand the hierarchies across key jurisdictions, it seems sensible to consider options for even further clarity, such as common 'flags' indicating where instruments sit in the hierarchy.
- Thirdly, 'no creditor worse off' is not yet clear: differing insolvency regimes make the valuation very difficult in practice. Regulators should work with independent valuers to develop a workable policy solution.

Deutsche Bank is a strong supporter of the Banking and the Capital Markets Union within the EU. If the challenges outlined here can be overcome, future resolution cases would likely benefit.

Where does the EU stand relative to the US?

In the aftermath of the financial crisis, the US authorities have had a head start and have also gained substantial experience from the closure and resolution of banks. The Single Resolution Mechanism (SRM), which was established on January 1, 2016, has quickly progressed work on the European regulatory framework, for example by developing banks' resolution plans and communicating MREL targets.

In this respect, it is worth noting that the progress made to date has been an invaluable exercise. In responding to resolution requests, banks have further improved their business-as-usual (BAU) processes. European banks are now better capitalized, have increased liquidity reserves, and reduced balance sheets. The industry is far more transparent and resilient than before the crisis. The benefits of this considerable and successful joint effort between the banks and the authorities cannot be overstated.

Nevertheless, the EU resolution authorities should consider increasing the level of information available to individual banks, as well as in the public domain, in a manner similar to that which exists in the US. Such transparency can substantially foster both ex-ante trust and the effectiveness of resolution planning since the latter is generally dependent on other authorities, counterparties and clients acting rationally during a resolution event.

Conclusion

The BRRD has provided positive groundwork within the EU for a strong resolution framework and banks themselves have made significant progress towards achieving successful recovery and resolvability. However, the work here is not yet complete. Further integration of the European Banking Union will support finalization. This is vital to ensure best preparation and to have the highest probability of minimizing the negative effects of a resolution of a GSIB on European taxpayers, its economy or the single currency.

However, whilst banks themselves can be operationally prepared for a resolution, this preparation only goes as far as the 'four walls' of the institution. Other vital market participants must ensure they have the same level of preparedness, for example exchanges must be able to facilitate the large volume of debt-equity swaps we would expect to see in a bail-in. Furthermore, there are still many open policy questions on the table that are yet to be progressed. These include the role of the independent valuer in resolution and the need to have, ex-ante, data production to support the valuations required by the BRRD, the mechanism for converting debt to equity, and finally the ability of banks, particularly within the Banking Union, to access liquidity in resolution.

Patrick Kenadjian

Open questions on bank resolution in Europe

Introduction

Despite all of the progress made in the European Union (the EU) to develop and implement a comprehensive system for providing governments with an alternative between bailing out financial institutions and allowing them to fail in a disorderly manner, including Directive 2014/59/EU on recovery and resolution of credit institutions and investment firms, commonly referred to as the Bank Recovery and Resolution Directive (BRRD) and the Minimum Requirement for Own Funds and Eligible Liabilities (MREL), there remain a number of nagging doubts about both the commitment of at least parts of the EU to bail-in over bail-out with the use of public funds and the effectiveness of the BRRD, perched as it is atop national laws differing on issues ranging from the ranking of debt obligations to procedural and substantive insolvency rules.

The doubts as to commitment focus primarily on Italy. Whatever else happens on the resolution front in the rest of the EU, there is a widespread perception that the rules in Italy seem to be different. Fingers are pointed at Italy principally in connection with the liquidation of two banks in Northern Italy (the Veneto Banks) and the precautionary recapitalization of the world's oldest bank, Monte dei Paschi di Siena (MPS). The two present very different issues from which I think different conclusions should be drawn.

I think the more important of the two from a policy point of view is MPS where use was made of a loophole in the EU State Aid rules provided in the BRRD which the Commission was supposed to review and report on to the European Parliament and the Council by December 31, 2015, but which it failed to do. The case of the Veneto Banks raises the question of the distinction made by the Single Resolution Board (SRB) between their case, in which the SRB found no public interest to justify a resolution, and the case of Banco Popular Español (Banco Popular), a bank with a similar mix of business, where it found the requisite public interest. Presumably size must have played a role, as Banco Popular was much larger than the Veneto Banks combined, but no public statement explaining the distinction was made. I will deal with these issues in points 1–3 below.

Patrick Kenadjian, Senior Counsel, Davis Polk & Wardwell LLP

https://doi.org/10.1515/9783110644067-005

Two further issues concern problems particular to the BRRD, those related to the independent expert valuations required before certain actions can be taken and whether the BRRD can be successfully implemented sitting atop very different national laws. I will deal with in points 5, 6 and 7 below.

Other open issues are common to resolution regimes in the US and Europe in particular who is to provide liquidity in a resolution, which I deal with in point 4, how much progress has been made in ensuring resolvability through the preparation of resolution plans, which I deal with in point 7 and what restrictions should be placed on who can hold bail-inable debt, which I will deal with in point 8.

1 The Veneto Banks special insolvency

We all understand that resolution, both under Title 2 of the Dodd-Frank Wall Street Reform and Consumer Protection Act (DFA) in the US and the BRRD was always meant to be the exception and not the rule, and that normal bankruptcy or insolvency proceedings should be the norm for insolvent financial groups.[1] And yet, when the SRB determined on June 23, 2017 that in the case of the Veneto Banks which their primary supervisor, the European Central Bank (ECB) had determined were "failing or likely to fail" (FOLTF), having repeatedly breached supervisory capital requirements, the conditions for resolution were not met because there was no public interest justifying resolution action and referred the Veneto Banks to the Banca d'Italia, in its capacity as Italian National Resolution Authority, to wind them down under "normal insolvency proceedings", the actions taken under the Banca d'Italia's aegis prompted a flurry of complaints that Italy was again testing EU rules and creating a "two-speed Eurozone".

The situation in which the Veneto Banks found themselves, still alive after so many years of losses, is clearly a result of forbearance, born of the reluctance to impose losses on retail investors holding subordinated debt and to the extent that retail subordinated debt holders were exempted from write-downs, that too would be forbearance, although that is complicated by the issue of mis-selling those instruments. However, what the Banca d'Italia actually did looked very much like a traditional Federal Deposit Insurance Corporation (FDIC) operation, whereby the two banks were wound down with the transfer of the performing assets and related liabilities to a solvent bank (Intesa San Paolo) and the transfer of the non-

1 For US banks, the rule is different. They are expected to be taken over by the Federal Deposit Insurance Corporation ("FDIC") under the FDIC Act in an administrative process which is the model for resolution regimes adopted since the great financial crisis.

performing assets to a vehicle used in a previous liquidation, Atlante, together with the claims of the banks' shareholders and subordinated debt holders. It also looked a lot like the use of the transfer of business resolution tool under the BRRD, since the good assets and related liabilities were transferred without consent of the counterparties or the banks' shareholders. It also involved "state aid", as the acquiring bank received a cash injection of €4.785 billion from the Italian Treasury, including €3.5 billion to maintain its capital ratios and its dividend policy(!) unchanged and €1.285 billion to cover staff layoffs and branch closures as well as state guarantees estimated at €12 billion related to the financing of the liquidation procedure. While this may look like a rather generous package, it did not involve payments to the banks' existing creditors or shareholders, but to the bank acquiring their good assets to induce them to continue operating them. This aid was duly approved by the European Commission the day it was granted, on June 25, 2017. *See* EU Directorate-General for Internal Policies (IPOL) Economic Governance Support Unit (EGOV) Briefing to the European Parliament on the orderly liquidation of Veneto Banca and Banco Populare di Vicenza, PE 602.094 (2017).

The decree law which allowed the Banca d'Italia to take these actions actually stated that "normal" insolvency proceedings would – contrary to the SRB's finding – cause great damage to the Italian economy, thus the recourse to the "special" insolvency procedures tantamount to the use of resolution tools. So, basically what happened was that the competent resolution authority, the SRB, found no public interest justifying a resolution and the National Resolution Authority, to whom it referred the matter for disposition, the Banca d'Italia, disagreed and took action equivalent to resolution to prevent the destruction of value and serious losses for retail unsecured creditors and the cessation of the credit relationships for businesses and families. This sounds like a difference of views on what constitutes the public interest and the Commission approved substantial state aid in connection with the Banca d'Italia's actions. The SRB's view was that neither bank provided critical functions, since their services were provided to a limited number of third parties and could be replaced in an acceptable manner and within a reasonable timeframe, and that their failure was not expected to have significant impact on financial stability, given the low interconnectedness of the banks with other financial institutions, and that normal insolvency proceedings would provide the same level of protection for depositors, investors, customers and clients' assets and funds. *See* PE 602.094.

The SRB was able to conclude that normal Italian insolvency proceedings would provide the same level of protection for investors, customers and clients' assets and funds as resolution because Italian insolvency law includes a special chapter called "forced administrative liquidation" to deal with banks and other financial institutions which provides for an administrative procedure quite close to resolution. So the key issue I see is the conclusion by the SRS that deposit taking from households and SMEs and lending activities to SMEs are not critical functions, at least not where the institution involved is below a certain size. Here the two institutions combined (and they were planning to merge) had total assets of €62.5 billion. Size must have had something to do with the decision, since the SRB cited deposit taking from households and non-financial corporations (SMEs) and lending to SMEs as part of the public interest justifications for approving the resolution of Banco Popular Español on June 7, 2017. For reference, the Banco Popular balance sheet the SRB was looking at was €148 billion, so there was a significant difference in size. Nonetheless, as Andrea Enria, at the time Chair of the European Banking Authority (EBA), noted in an interview, "the decision that there was no EU public interest at stake in the crises of two ECB-supervised banks that were hoping to merge and operate in the same region with combined activities around €60 billion sets the bar for resolution very high." *See* PE 602.094, p.7. This strikes me as an issue worthy of more public debate than I think it has received, rather than one which should be left to an ad hoc decision taken by a resolution authority acting in a crisis under time pressure. General guidelines would promote predictability and add to the felt legitimacy of resolution decisions.

But the real reason for the Italian state to step in and for the Commission to agree to the aid may in fact be related less to critical functions than to the consequences of a collapse of these two banks. According to reports in the Italian press, the fear was the damage to the underfunded Italian deposit insurance fund which would not have been large enough to cover the losses had the Veneto Banks failed, leading to capital calls from all Italian banks potentially large enough to drain their capital buffers and thus lead to further banking failures, bank runs and a drag on economic performance, so both a serious disruption and a threat to financial stability. If this is true, the real problem was the failure to follow through on a European Deposit Insurance Scheme (EDIS) the so-called third pillar of the Banking Union, which would have more easily been able to absorb the losses involved.

2 The use of precautionary recapitalization in the case of MPS

What does smack of forbearance is the handling of MPS, in which on July 4, 2017 the European Commission approved the precautionary recapitalization via capital injection by the Italian state of €3.9 billion, plus €1.5 billion to compensate retail investors who were victims of mis-selling, for a total of €5.4 billion in state aid. The transaction also involved the conversion of junior bond holders for €4.3 billion and the transfer of a €26.1 billion portfolio of non-performing loans to a private securitization vehicle.

MPS had signally failed the EBA's 2016 EU-wide stress test of banks, being the only bank whose result under the adverse scenario was actually negative (a fully-load CET1 ratio at December 31, 2015 of – 2.44%). This failure was followed by further losses in the second half of 2016, as a result of which MPS agreed with the ECB to raise €5 billion from investors, but was only able to raise €1 billion. The ECB subsequently raised its assessment of MPS's capital shortfall by €3.8 billion. However, MPS claimed it was still solvent because it met its current Pillar 2 requirement and the €8.8 billion shortfall related to a fully loaded 8.1% CET 1 capital shortfall, i.e. to a level of capital it was not yet required to hold. Thus MPS had badly failed an adverse scenario stress test which was a hypothetical scenario, was unable to raise capital, but was not currently below its Tier 1 capital requirements, despite having made significant losses in every year but one since 2011 and having a non-performing loan (NPL) ratio of over 33% and a capital impairment ratio (unreserved impaired loans over equity) of over 285%. So it was deemed eligible for a precautionary recapitalization under the BRRD.

Article 32(4)(d)(iii) of the BRRD provides for the possibility of public support for weak but viable banks through "an injection of own funds or purchase of capital instruments ... of a precautionary and temporary nature" where necessary to remedy a serious disturbance in the economy of a Member State and preserve financial stability. The measures must be of a precautionary and temporary nature, proportionate to remedy the consequences of the serious disturbance and may not be used to offset losses incurred or likely to be incurred. The clause was added relatively late in the drafting process of the BRRD and it was unclear whether it was intended itself to be limited in time or to be a permanent part of the bank crisis management toolkit.

The arguments for a temporary fix are clearly the stronger. The first is the requirement in Article 32 itself that the Commission review whether there is a continuing need for it and report back to the European Parliament and the Council by December 31, 2015. Beyond that, we are currently in a transition period with regard to resolution in the EU. Bank balance sheets still contain relatively high levels of NPLs related to lending in the run up to the great financial crisis of 2008/2009 and the subsequent Euro-zone crisis, but the structures of resolution under the BRRD, and especially the requirements for MREL, which is meant to insure that institutions will have sufficient bail-inable debt so that they will not be required to be bailed out, are not yet fully in place. Other elements of bank regulation are also only slowly settling into place, with final agreement on the Basel III capital requirements having only been reached in December 2017 and still needing to be implemented locally. Therefore an argument can be made that until we are over this transition period, at least until the levels of MREL for the individual banks have been set and that MREL has been put in place, an instrument like precautionary capitalization can be justified, so long as the Commission is satisfied that the state aid element is justified and the bank is viable.

The argument for making precautionary recapitalization a permanent feature of the BRRD strikes me as harder to sustain, although my friend Nicolas Véron ably marshals the arguments in favor of it in his in-depth analysis of the problem for the European Parliament dated 11 July 2017. *See* Precautionary recapitalizations: time for a review, IPOL EGOV PE 602.090, July 2017. His strongest argument is that the US escaped disaster in 2008/09 because Congress was able to pass the TARP legislation in a matter of days, but that prompt legislative action in the EU (and he could also have added the US) today is highly unlikely and thus that it would be foolish to eliminate a safety valve which might allow decisive actions on a timely basis in a crisis.

I clearly see the point, but I see a greater problem in keeping it, in that it allows an ill-defined exception to the general rule and while that may well give resolution authorities and the Commission welcome flexibility in a given case, it will also tend to call into question the predictability of the system. So long as it is there, can investors, depositors and the public be sure we have moved from the bad old bail-out days to the bright and shiny new bail-in regime? And if there is a doubt, what incentive do bank managements have to clean up their balance sheets and what disciplinary function can the market exercise on them? It is clear that the drafters of the BRRD had doubts about creating a permanent loophole, in that the BRRD asks the Commission to review its continued necessity and submit a report by the end of 2015. The Commission has so far failed to do so. One can surmise that they like the flexibility it gives them. And because state aid is involved, the decision is the Commission's and the Commission's alone to make. This can be useful in a systemic crisis, but also as part of a political accommodation with an important Member State government. The text itself is full of potential contradictions which make it, to my mind, hard to apply. For example, the aid cannot be used to offset losses either incurred or likely. How do you apply that when you are repairing the balance sheet of an institution which has been diminished by prior losses and where future losses are likely? The aid also cannot confer an advantage on the institution, although it is bolstering its capital in a way the market has refused to do. Finally, the balance between the aid and the disturbance is not an analysis I have seen in any of the cases Nicolas cites, including MPS.

In the end, however, as so often, I do agree with him in his conclusion that if the Commission wanted to limit the use of precautionary recapitalization, it would not even need to go so far as deleting or amending Article 34(d)(iii) of BRRD. It is open to the Commission to limit its use simply by tightening its state aid criteria. The issue there is the definition of "a serious disturbance in the economy of a member state" under Article 107(3)(b) of the Treaty on the Functioning of the European Union (TFEU). How widespread and severe must a "serious disturbance" be to qualify? Is it sufficient if one large city or any important region is affected? The only problem I see with this solution is that it leaves the question in the hands of an agency, the Directorate General for Competition (DG Comp) whose job is the preservation of competition, not financial stability and while DG Comp has done an admirable job in reining in state aid since the financial crisis, the whole idea of resolution is to put decisions in the hands of agencies tasked with preserving financial stability.

3 How well does resolution work under BRRD: The case of Banco Popular

So far we have one real poster child for the proposition that resolution under the BRRD works, at least for idiosyncratic bank failures, Banco Popular in which on June 7, 2017 the SRB applied the sale of business tool to sell it to Banco Santander, and exercised the power of write down and conversion of capital instruments, to write down to zero all of the bank's common shares and Additional Tier 1 instruments and converting its Tier 2 instruments into shares which were sold to Santander for €1.

Several aspects of this transaction are worth noting. First, the bank was deemed failing or likely to fail, not because of a capital shortfall, but because it ran out of liquidity, despite having a liquidity coverage ratio (LCR) at December 31, 2016 of 134.8% of the fully phased in LCR requirement for 2018, and despite having sought and obtained emergency liquidity assistance (ELA) from the Banco de España in the amount of €3.6 billion. I will return to the issue of liquidity in point 4 below.

Second, several elements of the timing are interesting. Much has been made of the claim that "we did this not even over a weekend, but from a Tuesday to a Wednesday" to show that resolution under the BRRD can be made to work effectively. But what this really means is that the bank's situation deteriorated so quickly that it could not survive until the weekend even though it was clearly being closely watched by the SRB and the Spanish resolution authority (FROB).

The "valuation 2" report provided to the SRB by an independent expert which I will discuss further below under point 5 tells us that the expert was mandated to provide the report 12 days before and at the time agreed to a timetable of six weeks to conduct their review. This shows the SRB was on the case, but that its timetable ended up being overtaken by events. In fact, the FROB has stated that the SRB had on June 3 instructed it to commence an auction proceeding to sell the bank. Thus, the bank was in the midst of trying to sell itself and interested buyers already had access to a data room and were performing due diligence on the bank, so that when its liquidity deteriorated there was already a bidder in the wings. The "independent expert", the accountancy firm Deloitte, was able to perform in record time the provisional valuation required by Article 36.4 of the BRRD before the SRB could use the sale of asset tool and the bail-in tool, and also to determine that no creditor of the bank was worse off than under liquidation (NCWO) as required by Article 36 of the EBRD. This is a process which, as we will discuss more fully below under point 7, the Bank of England has estimated would normally require months rather than days, but was here performed in a remarkably swift manner. The FROB, to whom the actual resolution steps were delegated, notes the valuation ranged from an adjusted equity of negative €8.2 billion in an adverse (worst case) scenario to a negative €2 billion in a baseline (best estimate) scenario. Somewhere, lost in the shuffle, was also a positive €1.3 billion "best case" equity estimate, though it is unclear what we are to make of this, as it is not otherwise discussed. *See* Deloitte, Hippocrates Provisional Valuation Report, [Sale of Business Scenario], 6 June 2017, p.2.

Thus, without wanting to take away any credit from the remarkable job the SRB did in this case, it must be said that it benefited from a happy set of circumstances, which allowed it to find a willing buyer already on the spot. It should also be noted that, unlike Intesa San Paolo, which received significant state aid to take over the good business of the Veneto Banks, Santander received no such payments. In fact, it went out and raised an additional €7 billion in capital on its own to cover additional provisioning at Popular. So this was a truly clean bail-in plus sale of assets. So, if we are lucky we can hope to see resolution work in the case of an idiosyncratic bank failure, where all energy can be focused on a single bank in crisis.

This does not mean that in a systemic crisis, with multiple fires to put out and therefore multiple sources of contagion to the financial system, we can expect to be so lucky. It is unlikely that all of the institutions involved will have an up to date on-line data room (although, on reflection, requiring such a data room, at least for globally significant financial situations as part of their resolution planning, while somewhat burdensome, would not be a bad idea) and equally unlikely are willing buyers who have done at least part of their homework. Moreover, in a situation which smells of systemic crisis even the most decisive of CEOs may hesitate to engage in an acquisition where the extent of the liabilities to be assumed is likely to be less than clear. In times of Knightian uncertainty, buyers tend to become scarce. Finally, with assets of under €150 billion, Popular was large enough to warrant resolution, but not too large for Santander to absorb. If it had been a bank the size of Santander with assets of close to €500 billion that was in distress, where would the buyer large and stable enough to acquire it have been found?

The Banco Popular case also highlighted two different issues, one common to all resolutions, of who provides the liquidity in a resolution and one peculiar to resolutions under the BRRD, whether its requirement the multiple valuations be undertaken makes the system unworkable, which I shall address next.

4 Who provides liquidity in resolutions under the BRRD?

As the liquidity crisis which tipped Banco Popular into resolution makes clear, liquidity is likely to be a key issue in a bank resolution, as it is in any insolvency. As noted above, Popular was more than in compliance with the Basel LCR Rules on liquidity, but still appears to have suffered a classic bank run with large depositors, apparently including the public sector, withdrawing large amounts of deposits which must have exceeded its estimates of its liquidity needs for 30 days. It was also unable to come up with enough collateral to support its requests for ELA from the Bank of Spain. There are conflicting accounts concerning the haircuts which the ECB – whose consent is required for a Member State central bank, such as the Bank of Spain, to grant ELA above a relatively low threshold – may or may not have imposed on the collateral Banco Popular was able to present (some Spanish press reports imply haircuts of up to 90%), but it would not be surprising to find that an institution whose business model concentrated on real estate and SME lending would encounter steep haircuts in presenting such assets to a central bank as collateral. Nonetheless, this raises two important pre-resolution questions. First, how adequate are the current LCR rules in providing the needed liquidity and how well are they being enforced by bank supervisors? Second, how well is liquidity planning being integrated into banks' recovery and resolution plans?

But the real problem for resolution in the EU is that, in contrast to the Dodd Frank Act in the US (DFA) where the Federal Deposit Insurance Corporation has what amounts to an open line of credit from the US Treasury to provide liquidity in an orderly liquidation procedure under Title II of DFA or to Chapter 11 of the US Bankruptcy Code where lenders to an institution in bankruptcy are entitled to a super priority claim on the institution's estate for any credit extended during a bankruptcy proceeding, under the BRRD there is no specific mechanism for dealing with liquidity during resolution. Some independent central banks outside the Euro system, such as the Bank of England, have made clear that they will provide the necessary liquidity. The Bank of England has stated in its famous "purple book" that firms in resolution continue to have access to its ordinary liquidity facilities, supplemented, if needed, by a flexible Resolution Liquidity Framework, "designed to provide liquidity, in sterling or foreign currency, in the necessary scale, for a sufficient period of time, and secured against a wide range of collateral," where the institution is subject to a Bank of England led resolution, but not where someone else is leading the resolution. (*See* The Bank of England's approach to resolution, October 2017, p.22). The formulation is clearly intended to reassure the market that liquidity support will be available in sufficient quantity (somewhat reminiscent of Mario Draghi's "and believe me, it will be enough") so as to discourage a run and encourage post resolution lenders to make private funds available. However, as a practical matter, the question of adequate collateral may well remain.

The situation within the Euro system is not as clear. And this is one issue on which the normally very reliable Financial Stability Board has until recently been less helpful than usual. Their approach is that the institution to be resolved and the market must in the first instance provide and that the public sector i.e. the central banks or the national treasuries should only provide a backstop. *See* Financial Stability Board, Guiding principles on the temporary funding needed to support the orderly resolution of a global systemically important bank (G-SIB), 18 August 2016, pages 9–12. I fear this is not realistic, but the path the Euro system is following seems to me even more tentative. Member State central banks, such as the Bank of Spain, may grant ELA, but only to the extent permitted by the ECB and Banco Popular's case reminded us that those conditions could be quite restrictive depending on the types of collateral the institution in resolution has to offer. It would clearly be preferable if the BRRD or the ECB made clear ex ante what degree of liquidity support resolution authorities may count on to sustain institutions during a resolution. This would be consistent with the FSB's recommendation of an effective public sector backstop funding mechanism. However, the issues with available collateral in the midst of what may turn out to be a bank run also mean that the ECB would likely need some specific statutory direction to derogate from its usual rules on collateralized lending if it was to intervene effectively here. Absent this kind of specific mandate I see a problem there.

None of the resolution tools the BRRD provides generates liquidity. The power to write down or convert debt or equity helps clear up the institution's balance sheet but does not provide one cent of liquidity. The power to sell assets likewise cannot be expected to generate liquidity since those asset sales are generally paid for by the assumption of liabilities rather than the payment of cash, beyond a token €1. And while there is something called the Single Resolution Fund (SRF), its amount, when fully funded, in 2024, it will be limited to €55 billion, or 1% of covered deposits. While the SRF may call upon additional ex post contributions, to a total of €75 billion, at July 19, 2017 it had only collected €17 billion and it is not clear that it can actually be used to provide liquidity support during a resolution. While one of its permitted uses is to make loans to an institution under resolution, the SRF can only be used after 8% of the institution's liabilities have been bailed in and is limited to 5% of the institution's total liabilities. *See* SRB, what is the Single Resolution Fund? available on the SRB's website. Both these limitations are likely to make the use of the SRF to fund liquidity difficult. The general consensus among commentators appears to be that the SRF will be used for capital measures and that liquidity support will have to come from elsewhere.

The consequence of all of this is that, in the absence of additional clarity on the availability of liquidity in resolution, within the Eurozone resolution authorities as a practical matter may only be able to use those tools provided by the BRRD which get rid of the problem quickly, so that the institution is not left in their hands, as it might be if they decided to create a bridge bank and operate it for a while. This is what Klaus Knot, Governor of the Dutch Central Bank, has referred to as "the elephant in the room called 'Fury', or funding in resolution" in a speech delivered at the annual SRB conference in Brussels in 2017. *See* Klaus Knot, Pendulums and pitfalls on the road to resolution, 29 September 2017. In his speech he points out the gap between resolution planning under the BRRD, which explicitly excludes taking the possibility of extraordinary liquidity support into consideration, the availability of ELA only up until resolution and the awkward situation of an institution in resolution which may need liquidity the market is unable or unwilling to supply and also be unable to meet the normal collateral requirements for access to central bank liquidity at a time when eligible collateral can be expected to have already been pledged for other purposes. Even in a situation where resolution is not triggered by a liquidity shortfall as was the case for Banco Popular, liquidity planning during a resolution seems to be an aspect of resolution to which additional attention should be devoted. It is one to which the US Federal Reserve is devoting increased attention and Elke Koenig of the SRB has been quoted as viewing the provision of liquidity to a bank in crisis as one of the most pressing problems in resolutions. *See* Alexander Weber, EU banks told to get crisis-ready by removing wind-down hurdles, last published Dec. 17, 2017 livemint.

This is an issue to which, to their credit, both the ECB and the SRB have recently turned their attention, both in public appearances and, if the press is correctly informed, in the form of a still confidential ECB proposal to establish a Eurosystem Resolution Liquidity (ERL) facility. The FSB has also focused on the centrality of funding in resolution in its recent Funding Strategy Elements of an Implementable Resolution Plan of 21 June 2018. And finally, the issue has been taken to the attention of the European Parliament. *See* IPOL EGOV Briefing on the Banking Union: Towards new arrangements to finance banks under resolution? July 2018 and related in-depth analyses, especially Alexander Lehmann, Cash outflows in a crisis: do liquidity requirements and reporting obligations give the SRB sufficient time to react? April 2018.

Lehmann's paper provides valuable background on the historical importance of liquidity support in past crises. But the essential point that the EU needs a clear path to the provision of liquidity in resolution seems to have been taken up by all concerned and while there are numerous issues to be resolved, including whether liquidity should be provided by the ECB or should continue to be funneled through the national banks as with ELA and how the central bank providing liquidity can best be protected against losses on such lending, including whether guarantees might replace the need for collateral, there has been much positive movement since Yves Mersch's rather discouraging speech at this University on January 30, 2018 in which he laid out all the obstacles to the ECB's involvement in resolution financing. *See* Yves Mersch, The limits of central bank financing in resolution, IMFS Distinguished Lecture Series, Goethe University Frankfurt, 30 January 2018. It seems that the days of "constructive ambiguity" about liquidity support, a policy fueled by central bank fears of moral hazard, have passed and that the benefits of greater certainty in reducing the risk of fire sales of assets causing contagion have been recognized. It is clear we are far from having solved the problem. The European Parliament July 2018 Briefing cited above and an excellent research report by BBVA Research, Funding before and in resolution, A proposal for a funding in resolution mechanism, 31 May 2018 set out the numerous issues to be resolved. Nonetheless, since the date of our conference, we do seem to be making progress.

5 Valuations and transparency

The BRRD requires that three different valuations be made in connection with a resolution. The first, the so-called valuation 1, is conducted under standard accounting procedures and regulatory capital requirements on a going concern basis and is required to determine whether the financial institution is failing or likely to fail. This is the June 5, 2017 analysis the SRB made of Banco Popular described immediately above in point 6. The second, the so-called valuation 2, is the one Deloitte performed which we discussed in point 3 above on the basis of which the resolution tools, in this case bail-in and transfer of business, are chosen. It is based on the present value of expected future cash flows, on a going concern basis. These are required by Article 36 of the BRRD. The third, the so-called valuation 3, is required under Article 74 of the BRRD and is meant to determine whether any of the institution's creditors are worse off as a result of resolution than they would have been in an ordinary insolvency (the NCWO standard) and is conducted on a going concern basis. As noted above, Deloitte took a stab at that valuation in its valuation 2 opinion as well. This part of their report was so severely redacted, removing all useful numbers, that it was all but impossible to understand the basis for their calculations. It was somewhat surprising to me to see this valuation 3 attempt so early in the game. I would have expected it to come later, after the resolution had been completed, as provided in Article 74(1). In fact that valuation 3 report did appear a year later, dated June 12, 2018. *See* Deloitte, Valuation of difference in treatment, Banco Popular Español, issued as at 12 June 2018. In any event, the June 2017 effort has, predictably, been labeled as flawed by representatives of the holders of Tier 1 and Tier 2 capital instruments of Banco Popular which were written down or converted into the shares sold to Santander for €1, and Deloitte itself qualified its June 2017 conclusions as "highly uncertain". The problems were predictable from the beginning and I have labeled them as likely source of litigation, if not a hold-up for the Resolution process in prior books in this ILF series. So far, they have not proven capable of holding up the process, which is good news, but the problems are baked into the process's timing since the BRRD requires there to be a valuation 1 to start the ball rolling and a valuation 2 to choose which resolutions tools to apply at the beginning of the process. If the tools chosen include bail-in, as is the general assumption and was the case in Banco Popular, the valuation 2 determination sets the initial loss holders of those instruments will bear, subject only to the possibility of some recovery under NCWO as the result of a valuation 3 study.

I have always been extremely skeptical about the ability of an independent expert to conduct a reliable valuation in the chaotic run up to a resolution action and agree heartily with the Bank of England's view that a proper valuation requires months, not days, to prepare. Deloitte apparently was initially given six weeks to conduct its valuation study, though in the end they had only 12 days, which they implicitly viewed as too short since their report highlights all the key information they were lacking. The Bank of England has designed an ingenious mechanism involving immobilizing MREL instruments at the relevant central securities depositaries and issuing tradeable certificates of entitlement instead which would be exchanged for final value once the valuation is completed. *See* Andrew Gracie, Making banks Resolvable: the key to making resolution work, Bank of England, 4 December 2017. I find the approach interesting, although perhaps not universally applicable. It seems to assume that all bail-inable debt, which may not be confined to MREL, can be found and immobilized. That may be a reasonable assumption for a G-SIB, especially in the UK or the US, but will it hold for smaller banks and in other markets?

On the other hand, I find the approach overall superior to other proposals, which seek to chip around the edges of the valuation problem and in doing so mix some useful and some potentially problematical suggestions. An excellent survey of what else could be done is to be found in Pieter de Goen's analysis prepared for the European Parliament and published in June 2018. *See* In-depth Analysis Requested by the ECON committee, Valuation reports in the context of banking resolution: what are the challenges? External author: Willem Pieter de Goen, IPOL EGOV, PE 624.418 June 2018. He rightly notes the broad range of values for Banco Popular found in Deloitte's valuation, from a positive €1.3 billion to a negative €8.2 billion with a best estimate (or should one say guess) of minus €2.0 billion, and he keenly analyses the information Deloitte acknowledged it was missing. This included not only critical information on the asset side, but also a detailed and reliable estimate of the creditor hierarchy. The latter was due to a lack of information on a legal entity level and on intragroup assets and liabilities, as well as the expected effects of the bank's deteriorating liquidity position on the structure of its liabilities. Serious attention needs to be given to these missing items to determine which could be remedied by a better designed resolution planning process and which are likely to be recurrent problems that can be expected to impair the accuracy and reliability of any valuation 2 exercise. In the case of the latter, what would that tell us about the vulnerability of such valuations to legal challenge? It is possible that the answer may simply be to treat incomplete valuations as preliminary, subject to completion when the missing information can be collected as suggested in BRRD Article 36(10).

Some of the solutions de Goen surveys are very sensible, such as those which focus on improving bank IT systems' ability to generate up to date and reliable information and to speed up the tender procedure for picking independent valuators. Others, while interesting, strike me as impractical, such as requiring the SRB to collect and make available to valuators very granular analyses of prior failures. While this kind of information is surely important for the SRB to understand, in particular how fast liquidity evaporates in a crisis (clearly Banco Popular's liquidity did), in view of the SRB's limited resources, the request to generate it should go to someone else. In the US this would be a job for the Financial Services Oversight Committee's well-staffed information arm, the Office of Financial Research. Finally, when he surveys proposals to impose moratoriums in resolution or the integrating of resolution procedures in Member State insolvency laws, we are moving to substantive changes in law to solve a procedural problem of our own making. While some of these proposals, e.g. harmonizing Member State insolvency laws, are quite desirable, adopting them to facilitate the valuation process is a bit like the tail wagging the dog. To his credit, he recognizes that moratoria can have severely disruptive effects and should be a last resort.

The valuations in Banco Popular highlight another problem, not with the BRRD itself, but with regard to transparency in the administration of resolutions. The valuations include sensitive data and the exercise of judgment concerning adjustments to value in highly uncertain circumstances. Hence a natural reluctance to expose that data to disclosure. But this leads to a bigger problem, which is in essence that analyzed by Paul Tucker in his admirable recent tome, Unelected Power, the Question of Legitimacy in Central Banking and the Regulatory State, Princeton University Press, 2018. Independent agencies to whom extensive powers are given to set policies which can have grave consequences for the well-being of large parts of the public need to conduct themselves in a way which allows the public to understand their processes and have faith in the way the public interest is being served. This goal cannot be reached by shrouding deliberations in secrecy and refusing to make public key documents related to the decisions taken. This is a lesson many older and tradition bound public institutions have had to learn. Central banks have learned they can no longer run along the old principle of "keeping the bank out of the press and the press out of the bank" and have changed to an approach of measured openness in what Chairman Powell of the US Federal Reserve has referred to as "a long march to transparency". Transparency is the prerequisite to accountability which is what gives these institutions democratic legitimacy. What works for the ECB, the Bank of England or the US Federal Reserve needs to apply to the SRB. The refusal to release any documents relating to the resolution of Banco Popular until forced to by its Appeals Panel at the behest of the holders of the bailed-in debt was what in US sports we would refer to as a "rookie mistake" which is part of the maturing process for public agencies and which we can hope will not be repeated. The same applies to releasing the documents it did release in heavily redacted form, similar to the approach taken by war time censors concerned about not revealing the location of their troops to those at home. One understands the motivations involved, but hopes the mistake will not be repeated. In fact, the actual Deloitte valuation 3 report in the form published a year later, was a model of transparency and disclosure.

Although the cover of the report notes that, in its published version, certain information has been redacted pursuant to Article 88 of Regulation (EU) No. 806/2014 to protect confidential information, redactions are in fact few and relate principally to the evaluation of legal contingencies. Otherwise the document is clear, complete and detailed. It concludes, unsurprisingly, that shareholders and creditors affected by the resolution actions would not have received more in a Spanish insolvency proceeding commenced on the date of the resolution action in June 2017 than they received in the resolution action.

6 Can the BRRD be made to work in the context of significant differences in Member State laws on insolvency, the hierarchy of debt and the treatment of collateral?

The BRRD refers in a number of places to the laws of the Member States to determine a number of key outcomes in resolution. The problem of course is that these laws differ substantially from one Member State to another so that outcomes the BRRD has implicitly assumed to be uniform may turn out to be anything but. The problems with a diversity of laws starts with the ranking of debt in insolvency, especially for MREL and TLAC, but extends to differences in insolvency procedures and speed, rules on collateral and other problems we have discussed before in connection with the difficulties in implementing the EU's Capital Markets Union project. *See* Andreas Dombret, Patrick S. Kenadjian (Eds.) The European Capital Markets Union, a viable concept and a real goal? (2015). The problems are in fact more acute in the resolution context because they go to two fundamental principles in resolution, that there should be ex ante clarity in the ranking of bank creditors and that of the NCWO guarantee the creditors whose rights are affected by write down or conversion in a resolution should not be worse off than in a normal insolvency. It has been proposed that this might be solved at the European level by the introduction of something like the proposed Chapter 14 of the Bankruptcy Code in the US, which would apply only to insolvencies of financial institutions. If not, is the only alternative that we must live with regional differences which will make the application of the BRRD different depending on the Member State? And if so, how valuable is the NCWO guarantee of the BRRD when the result will differ from one Member State to another?

As the authors of the Geneva Progress Report on Bail-ins and Resolution in Europe, Thomas Philippon and Aude Salord rightly point out in their March

2017 report, while constructive ambiguity as to which financial institution may be saved may be useful to alleviate moral hazard, there is nothing remotely constructive about ambiguity concerning the hierarchy of creditors within a bank. Efficiency requires that investors know where they stand in the hierarchy of creditors once resolution proceedings commence. Yet even something as crucial to resolution as the ranking of TLAC and MREL will generate different answers in Italy, Germany and France. This is all the more surprising to the outside observer that these differences were not there ex ante, but were created by specific legislation enacted to deal with bail-inable debt in a resolution context after adoption of the BRRD. Italy in 2015 contented itself with enacting a preference for deposits over other senior unsecured debt. The German Resolution Mechanism Act of November 2015 created with retroactive effect a super senior category for derivatives, collateralized bonds and structured notes. France created a new category of "senior non-preferred notes" for MREL and TLAC eligible debt without retroactive effect. *See* Thomas Philippon and Aude Salord, Bail-ins and Bank Resolution in Europe, A Progress Report, Geneva Reports on the World Economy Special Report 4, March 2017, pp.44–45.

Add to this differences in hierarchy under national insolvency laws and differences in laws on collateral. For example, under UK law the concept of fixed and floating charges is key to what collateral actually ends up securing a debt, where only the collateral available at the point where the floating change crystallizes is caught, but then rapidly. Contrast the situation in France where only assets initially specified are caught by the lien and realization may take years. Contrast again Germany where realization on collateral requires its transfer to the creditor.

The authors' suggestion is that creditor hierarchies should be incorporated into the BRRD and not be left to the national insolvency laws. The suggestion is an interesting one if it could in fact be done at the EU level so that changes would not need to be made in 28 different Member States. Whatever the route to greater clarity we take, it has to be clear that TLAC and MREL are subordinated at law if the whole bail-in structure is to work as advertised. The FSB's recommendations on TLAC include subordination. The same should apply to MREL.

The authors further suggest that consideration be given to a European equivalent of the proposed Chapter 14 to the US Bankruptcy Code which would apply to financial institutions, though they recognize this would require a difficult and lengthy process. At this point, it is probably worth opening a parenthesis concerning "Chapter 14". A concise description of the proposal in its current incarnation is to be found in the US Treasury's report to the President on OLA and bankruptcy reform. *See* The Department of the Treasury Report to the President of the United States Pursuant to the Presidential Memorandum Issued April 21, 2017, Orderly Liquidation Authority and Bankruptcy Reform, February 21, 2018, pages 23–28. Essentially, the idea is to allow a bank holding company to enter bankruptcy without affecting the operations of its operating subsidiaries whose shares, along with other operating assets and liabilities would be transferred to a newly formed bridge company, while its financial debt would stay behind. The shares of the bridge company would be held in trust for the holding company's shareholders and financial debt holders, who would be entitled to receive whatever the trustee realizes from the sale of the bridge company.

So Chapter 14 in essence involves the use of a bridge company to separate the claims of the shareholders and TLAC and other bail-inable debt holders from the banking operations of the group. This obviously assumes a holding company structure which is lacking in many parts of the EU. It also raises the question of liquidity financing for the bridge company, an issue still to be resolved, although the US may have two significant advantages over the EU in this area. The first is the concept of super priority for any lending to an institution in bankruptcy, which can be hoped to lead to private sector lending in resolution. The second is that the US requires resolution plans to calculate and provide for liquidity needs in resolution, so that financial groups interested in a bridge company solution should be working on that issue, whose importance the Federal Reserve has recognized. The FSB, in its June 2018 paper on funding strategy elements in resolution plans cited above, has also rallied to this side. It should be noted that much of what would be possible under Chapter 14, should it ever be adopted, can already be done under Chapter 11, as explained by David Skeel in his contribution to Making Failure Feasible. *See* David A. Skeel Jr., Financing Systematically Important Financial Institutions, in Kenneth E. Scott, Thomas H. Jackson, John B. Taylor, eds., Making Failure Feasible: How Bankruptcy Reform Can End "Too Big to Fail" (2015), pp. 63–65. Chapter 14 adds some useful bells and whistles to smooth the process and allows the US to live up to the preference for court supervised bankruptcy proceedings over administrative resolution.

Since Chapter 14 is largely predicated on the existence of a holding company structure, rather than what Diego Valiante refers to as a "big bank" structure in his study for the European Parliament on harmonizing insolvency laws in the Euro area (*See* European Parliament, Study Harmonising insolvency laws in the Euro Area: rationale, stock-taking and challenges. What role for the Eurogroup, External author: Diego Valiante, July 2016), a direct application of the Chapter 14 approach will not work in Europe, so another approach would have to be found. On the other hand, if in the absence of greater harmonization, a key protection for creditors in resolution, NCWO, can lead to very different results depending on where insolvency proceedings are opened, the effort to find another solution may be necessary. The Commission has already proposed a directive on preventive restructuring, insolvency and discharge procedures which would bring about considerable changes in Member State insolvency laws, importing many elements from the US Bankruptcy Code. Consideration of expanding that initiative to cover special provisions for the insolvency of financial institutions would seem worthwhile.

7 How much progress has been made in ensuring the resolvability of EU banking groups through the preparation of recovery and resolution plans?

Both statements of the SRB itself and the conclusions of the Special Report on the SRB by the European Court of Auditors (ECA) tend to corroborate the experience of G-SIBs subject to resolution planning on both sides of the Atlantic, that resolution planning has neither progressed as far not generated as much useful restructuring of financial groups as the resolution planning process has done in the United States under the DFA. The SRB emphasizes regularly that it is in a sense a "start-up" which has ramped up as quickly as possible to meet a herculean task. What it might add is that its job has been made considerably more difficult than it might have been by the decision made in Article 10 of the BRRD to task the SRB with drafting resolution plans for the banks, rather than reviewing drafts developed by the institutions themselves, with their incalculably vaster resources and knowledge of their internal structures, assets, liabilities, business plans, etc., as is the case with recovery plans which, under Article 5 of the BRRD are primarily the responsibility of the institutions themselves. In the US the institutions are primarily responsible for both plans, with resolution authorities saving their more limited resources to review both. As a result of this division of labor, several generations of resolution plans have been reviewed and sent back for reworking, putting corresponding pressure on the banks to improve their procedures or risk not only bad publicity when they are found not to be credibly resolvable, but also the ultimate sanction of being broken up if their plans fail to meet the authorities' standards three times.

Putting the burden to draft from scratch resolution plans for the 130 largest financial groups in the EU on a new institution which was established only in 2015 and is understaffed and underfunded seems like a recipe for assuring that what the Court of Auditors found in its December 2017 Special Report would occur. The ECA found that the SRB had been unable, among other things to evaluate impediments to resolution, set the individual levels of MREL or calculate the deductions therefrom. *See* European Court of Auditors, Special Report, Single Resolution Board: Work on a challenging Banking Union task started, but still a long way to go, December 2017. Deciding that MREL would be set on an institution by institution basis, rather than through application of a general rule, is yet another decision seemingly designed to slow down the process of resolution planning in the European Union. The SRB's MREL policy for 2017 called for MREL decisions to be communicated to a majority of global systemically important institutions (G-SIIs) in the first quarter of 2018, to be expanded to other systemically important institutions later in the year. This has apparently occurred in at least some cases, but not always resulted in public disclosure, probably because they contained no surprises.

The ECA's findings, which date back to 2017 and may relate to matters which have largely been remedied since, as indicated by Elke Koenig's more recent public statements (*See* Elke Koenig Speaks on Proportionality and MREL Implementation, Moody's Analytics, March 20, 2018) are nonetheless alarming for those of us who view resolution plans as the key component which protects the financial system against a repeat of the situation which faced Lehman Brothers' UK receivers in October 2008, walking in to a minefield of complexity with no map to guide them through the chaos. Further examples of what the ECA found were that the SRB had left many crucial components of the planning process unperformed, the division of labor between it and the national resolution authorities was unsettled, it had no framework for making its own determinations of whether a bank is failing or likely to fail and had conducted no simulation exercises ("dry runs") of resolution since 2016.

Some commentators, looking at the list of shortcomings, have been moved to wonder whether the SRB's apparent unpreparedness in 2016 and 2017 may have influenced what some have considered the ECB's arguably excessive reluctance to declare any bank failing or likely to fail in 2016 and 2017. *See* Nicolas Véron, Bad News and Good News for the Single Resolution Board, Blog Post January 15, 2018. In connection with the alleged inability to determine whether a bank is failing or likely to fail, an interesting document the SRB made public as a result of its Appeals Panel procedure in the Banco Popular case was an internal valuation conducted by the SRB on June 5, 2017, so on the eve of the ECB's determination that Banco Popular was failing or likely to fail, which came to the opposite conclusion. It is possible that the bank's situation deteriorated precipitously overnight, which in the case of liquidity squeezes is something we have seen happen before to the likes of Bear Stearns and Lehman Brothers, or that the SRB's evaluation was off. It is hard to know, from the outside, which is the case, especially since the SRB entirely redacted out the numerical part of its analysis.

8 What restrictions should there be on who can hold bail-inable MREL or TLAC debt

There are clearly two limitations here. First, it should not be held by other financial institutions whose position may be impaired if that debt is written down or cancelled and may put them in a position of having to sell any resulting equity they receive in a mandatory conversion for regulatory reasons. Secondly, it should not be held by unsophisticated individual investors who may be able to add a mis-selling claim to the institutions' other liabilities in a crisis or may be able to put political pressure on national resolution authorities to otherwise exempt or compensate them in case of a bail-in. On the latter issue, it is often argued that we allow individual investors to buy and hold equity, so why not a slightly more senior instrument? That argument misses the point that here we are not concerned about investor or consumer protection but about the availability of a determined amount of bail-inable debt to a financial institution in need of resolution. If it is there, the institution may be resolved. If it is not there because the holders can generate a counter claim for mis-selling or agitate successfully to be exempted, then the institution may not be resolvable after all. And should anyone need a real life example of this, they need only look to Italy, The forbearance that observers have noted in Italy is clearly related to the reluctance to force losses on retail holders of subordinated bank debt.

Conclusion

As Elke Koenig has often told us, resolution under the BRRD is not a product, it is a process and a process in progress at that. I think the European Union could be further along in this process had they made other decisions on who should draft resolution plans and how to set MREL and it would be desirable if the SRB could be staffed up so that some if its 2018/2020 work plan, in particular relating to the identification of obstacles to the resolution, could be brought forward, so that more banks are better prepared for a resolution crisis.

While I am heartened, and not surprised, by the strength of Deloitte's valuation 3 report of June 2018, which firmly demonstrates the unlikelihood of creditors and shareholders ultimately prevailing on NCWO claims, I still fear the valuation requirements will continue to be an open flank for creditors' suits and that additional thought should be given to creative solutions along the lines presented by the Bank of England in its "purple book" to allow a more thorough job to be done by the independent experts the first time around, to minimize the likelihood of NCWO adjustments post resolution.

I would favour a narrowing or elimination of the precautionary recapitalization loophole for the use of state aid as soon as possible. This could be done on a staggered basis, to be coordinated with the setting of binding MREL for banking groups or, at the latest, with the implementation date for the groups involved, i.e. starting with G-SIIs, moving on to O-SIIs and to the remaining groups.

But the main issue the European Union needs to address if it wants the full panoply of resolution tools provided for in the BRRD to be available in practice as well as in theory is to tackle the question of who provides liquidity in a resolution. Unless that is solved, resolution authorities are going to have to choose the tools that get the bank of their hands the quickest, not necessarily under the best conditions. The recent attention to this issue at the ECB and the European Parliament is a hopeful sign.

II Insurance Company Resolution

Felix Hufeld

Insurance company resolution – no need for additional European regulation

To safeguard the stability of the financial system and ensure the efficient resolution of failing banks, European supervisors and resolution authorities are committed to applying the EU Bank Recovery and Resolution Directive (BRRD) consistently and transparently across Member States.

The Key Attributes of Effective Resolution Regimes (KAs) developed by the Financial Stability Board (FSB) define rules especially for the resolution of global systemically important insurers (G-SIIs). In these KAs, the FSB sets out the core elements of an effective resolution regime. The objective of the KAs is the orderly resolution of financial institutions, i.e. including insurers, without endangering financial stability or placing a burden on the taxpayer.

The Insurance Core Principles (ICPs) of the International Association of Insurance Supervisors (IAIS) including the so-called Common Framework (ComFrame) provide further specific rules for the resolution of insurers.

Comparing apples and oranges

Comparing banking resolution and insurance resolution is like comparing apples and oranges; they are not really comparable. It is important to consider certain specific aspects of banking resolution and insurance resolution.

One of the key differences between banking and insurance resolution is the timeframe. When an insurer has problems that are potentially existential in nature, they usually become apparent at an early stage and the process therefore often starts even before recovery options are activated. The starting point is usually intensified supervision. This means that in the case of insurance undertakings such a situation does not usually occur overnight, so to speak. Another point that is often discussed in connection with the timeframe is the possibility of a “run”. Although a run on insurers is theoretically possible, it is much less likely to occur. This is especially true in the case of life insurance, given that cancellation periods need to be respected and the cancellation of an insurance contract before maturity usually entails deductions.

Felix Hufeld, President German Federal Financial Supervisory Authority (BaFin)

https://doi.org/10.1515/9783110644067-006

Another specific aspect is the existence of "critical functions" or "essential functions" which should be preserved in the case of resolution. As insurance functions are more readily substitutable, insurers are less likely to provide these "critical functions" or "essential functions".

And last but not least, the resolution of banks has to take special account of the fact that banks, unlike insurers, are institutionally connected to each other through the interbank market.

Debate on resolution rules for G-SIIs

With regard to the specific resolution rules for G-SIIs, there is currently a debate on whether systemic risk in the insurance sector should be looked at using an entity-based approach or if it is instead dependent more on the insurers' activities in the market as a whole, regardless of an individual insurer's size or interconnectedness.

The debate on how important insurers' activities are for systemic importance is reflected in the IAIS's work program, in which the organisation is developing a Holisitc Framework for systemic risk, that also includes the possibility for an identification of G-SIIs. This approach is designed to look at the systemic risk stemming from a number of insurance activities. It is important to note that failure is not necessarily required in such a situation, i.e. distress alone, coupled with the consequences thereof, can trigger contagion effects for the financial system and the real economy. The IAIS will start implementing the Holistic Framework beginning in 2020 and assess the implementation by 2022.

Furthermore, even though a single firm may not be able to have an impact on the wider financial system by itself, a number of insurers engaged in the same activity could, if they were affected the same way, have a systemic impact through their collective exposure.

Reinsurance and resolution

Reinsurance is a business to business activity and therefore needs to be looked at from a different perspective. The failure of a reinsurer does not have a direct impact on the policyholder in most cases and, in addition, reinsurance contracts usually run only for a short time period. The substitutability is therefore quite high in regional markets. Nevertheless, some core elements from the resolution rules for primary insurers might also be useful for reinsurance.

Run-off platforms

Another hot topic at the moment is the question of the role of run-off platforms in life insurance resolution. In times of distress of a life insurer, whether stand-alone or part of a larger insurance group, selling the existing portfolio of contracts or the whole company to a provider of specialised run-off services may be a viable option; in fact, it could help to safeguard policyholders' interests better and more successfully than if the contracts were to remain with the previous insurer. From a policyholder's perspective it is of paramount importance that the counterparty is solvent and appropriately managed, at least to the same extent as the previous counterparty. It is an important responsibility of the supervisor to closely monitor compliance with the legal requirements associated with such a transfer to protect policy holders' interests. Since in many jurisdictions, including Germany, such run-off platforms themselves have to be established as full-fledged (life) insurance companies both the legal act of transfering contracts as well as ongoing operations are subject to the same rules as any other insurance operation.

Differences from country to country...

To sum up, some elements have already been achieved at national level. Some countries, such as Germany, have already implemented many of the legal powers required by the FSB key attributes into their national supervisory insurance law. The implementation of further elements, for example regarding bridge institutions, still needs to be discussed. Germany is also applying existing Pillar II provisions on adequate risk management and Own Risk and Solvency Assessment (ORSA) processes, which should help insurance undertakings as well as operational supervisors to focus more consciously on the necessary recovery processes before any breach of Solvency Capital Requirement (SCR) key ratios occurs.

Differences exist from country to country, and these differences are justifiable. Insurance Guarantee Schemes (IGSs), which many Member States have had in place for quite some time, are a good example. These IGSs are in general adapted to the country's specific needs and are a core element in the relevant supervisory system.

...but no need for a legal structure at a European level

What we can see today is that there is no actual need to set up a separate legal structure for recovery and resolution requirements at a European level that are binding in all Member States, in a vein similar to that of the existing bank resolution regulation. With the adequate implementation of the FSB key attributes at national level, the existing measures for G-SIIs and the appropriate future-oriented application of existing Pillar II requirements on risk management and the ORSA we are at a good level.

This also means that it is not necessary to establish specific national insurance resolution authorities, because existing supervisory authorities can also be tasked with resolution. The important factor is the clear allocation of tasks and responsibilities between and within authorities.

Fausto Parente

Recovery, resolution and macroprudential policy in insurance – The need for European action

I Introduction

Following the financial crisis and the unprecedented public support to bail out failing financial institutions, the adequacy of crisis prevention and crisis management tools of national authorities has gained increasing attention. Although the majority of troubled institutions during the crisis were banks, insurers were also not immune to failure, as documented by EIOPA in a recent study concerning failures and near misses within the European insurance sector (EIOPA, 2018a).

As a result, newly developed concepts, such as recovery, resolution, macroprudential policy, etc. have emerged, as part of the vocabulary of policymakers and regulators alike. This has also triggered a debate on its applicability and an immense strand of work aimed at one main objective namely, to reduce the likelihood and the impact of any future crises, and the potential impact on the taxpayer. However, to date, the concept of an effective recovery and resolution regime remains not always well understood, particularly in insurance.

This article aims at contributing to the debate by arguing that a microprudential approach in the form of a recovery and resolution framework is needed for the insurance sector. It starts by providing an overview of cases of recovery and resolution of insurers in Europe. As a next step, it focuses on the policy proposal. Next, it considers a related issue, i.e. the need to supplement the current framework with a macroprudential approach. In its conclusion the article provides an indication on the work ahead.

Note: I would like to thank Juan Zschiesche and Josep Marquez for their valuable contributions in the preparation of this article.

Fausto Parente, Executive Director, European Insurance and Occupational Pensions Authority (EIOPA)

https://doi.org/10.1515/9783110644067-007

II Recovery and resolution in insurance

The financial crisis that severely impacted the banking sector in 2008 also put a considerable number of insurers under severe stress. The case of AIG is perhaps the most notorious one, but cases of insurance resolution or liquidation in Europe or overseas have not been rare or exceptional.

Up to now,[1] EIOPA's database of failures and near misses in insurance has recorded 87 relevant cases of (partial or total) resolution and liquidation of European[2] insurance undertakings since the year 2000, out of a total of 180 reported cases of failure and near misses.[3]

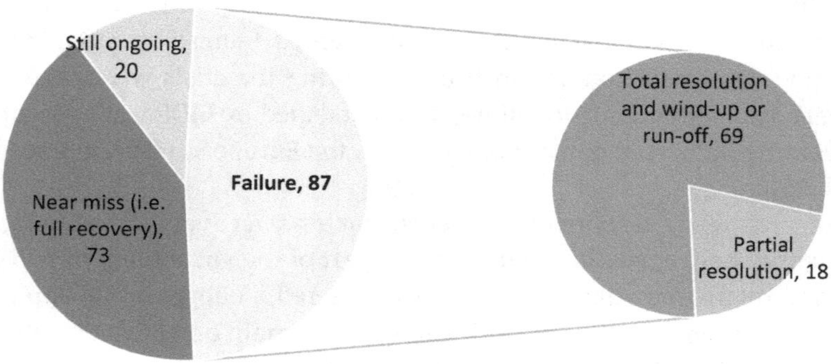

Figure 1: Outcome of the cases of failure and near miss in insurance.
Source: Based on EIOPA (2018a)

As depicted in relative terms in Figure 2, the 2008 financial crisis resulted, indeed, in a large number of failures and near misses in insurance, particularly in the case of those involved in the life and composite businesses. For instance, out of 51 distressed European Union life insurers registered in the

1 See EIOPA(2018a). National Supervisory Authorities (NSAs) were invited to report the most economically significant cases involving recovery and resolution of (re)insurers that had taken place at national level. An initial collection of data covered cases from year 2000 to 2014. Further updates were carried out covering cases during the years 2015 and 2016.

2 European Union (EU)/European Economic Area (EEA)

3 Partial resolution is considered when the insurer or a part of it managed to return to market after one or more resolution tools were used, or after receiving external financial support (be it in the form of public money or from funds coming from an IGS). In the cases of total resolution, the insurer was either liquidated or put in run-off.

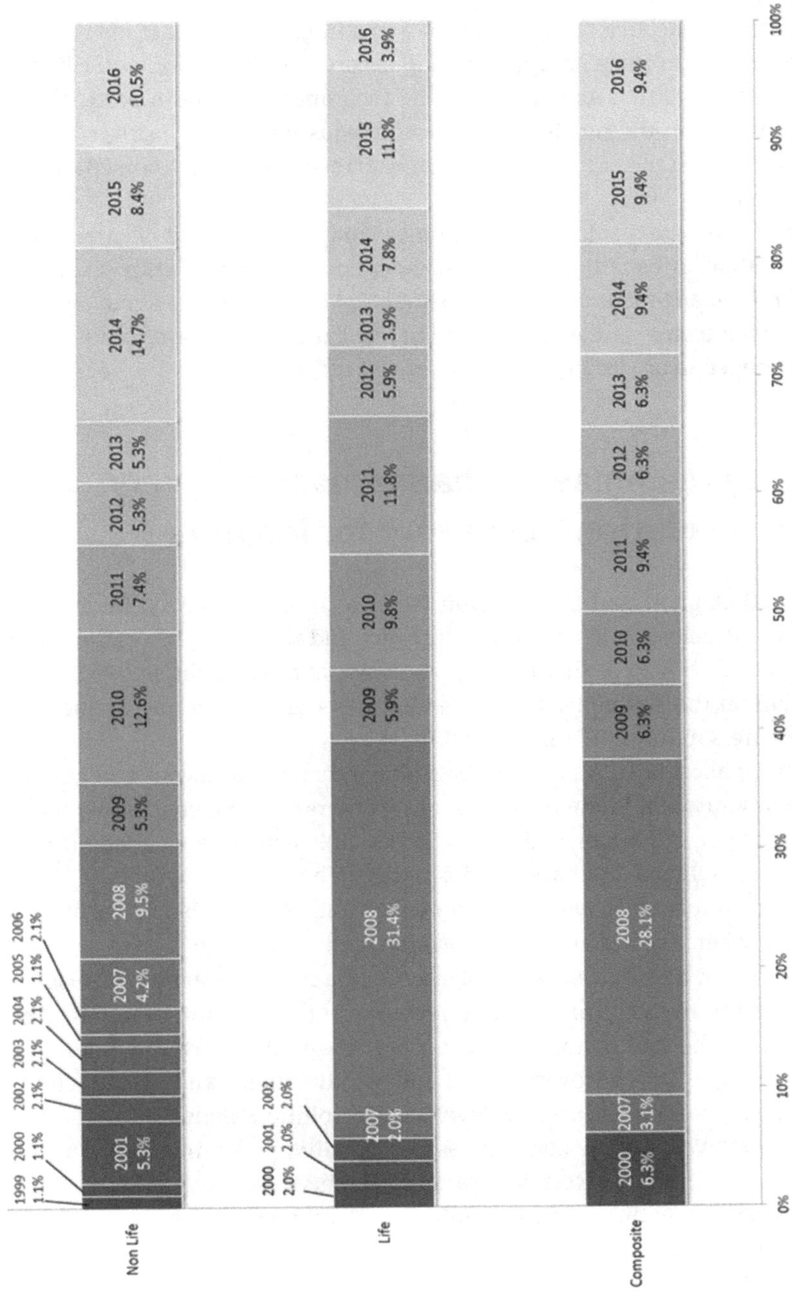

Figure 2: Split of the percentage of cases occurred per year, by type of insurer.
Source: EIOPA (2018a)

database as failures or near misses, about 37% were struck alone in the two-year period 2008–09.

The risk of collective failures occurring in a fragmented landscape was one reason for EIOPA to issue its Opinion on Recovery and Resolution published in July 2017 (EIOPA, 2017). As regards the life insurance segment in particular, it can be argued that the possibility of simultaneous failures of insurers cannot be ruled out, given the current challenging macroeconomic environment of low interest rates.

In summary, the resolution of insurance companies – albeit occurring less commonly than in banking – is not an exception nor an unknown phenomenon. Therefore, adequate mechanisms should be put in place to avoid such an undesirable outcome, while at the same time ensuring that the resolution process is managed in an orderly manner in case it indeed occurs.

III Policy responses: A harmonised recovery and resolution framework for insurers

In 2016, EIOPA published a Discussion Paper to receive feedback from stakeholders on all relevant issues around recovery and resolution. The Discussion Paper served EIOPA to further develop its views, and led to the publication of an Opinion on the Harmonisation of the Recovery and Resolution Framework for (Re)Insurers in July 2017 (EIOPA, 2017).

In the Opinion, EIOPA analysed both the arguments in favour and against further harmonisation in the field of recovery and resolution, concluding that a minimum degree of harmonisation should be implemented, which would help mitigate the likelihood and impact of insurance failures.

To achieve this objective, EIOPA proposed four building blocks for such a framework, where the definition of a common approach is key:

1. ***Preparation and Planning***: A harmonised framework should cover issues such as the need for pre-emptive recovery and resolution planning. The aim is, on the one hand, to reduce the probability of insurers failing by developing *ex ante* recovery plans, and, on the other hand, to reduce the impact of potential failures by developing resolution plans.
2. ***Early Intervention***: A common set of conditions for intervention and early intervention powers for National Supervisory Authorities (NSAs), the latter compatible with the Solvency II framework are required and have to be defined.

3. ***Resolution:*** A harmonised framework should consider relevant elements such as objectives for resolution, conditions or powers. EIOPA advises to clearly set out the objectives for resolution without ranking them. The protection of policyholders and financial stability should be part of the resolution objectives. Furthermore, EIOPA advises to include a common set of conditions for entry into resolution (trigger), based on the judgement and discretion of the resolution authority. EIOPA also proposes to broaden the existing resolution toolkit to introduce a common set of resolution powers with consistent design, implementation and enforcement features.
4. ***Cross-border Cooperation and Coordination Arrangements, including Exchange of Information:*** Cooperation structures between national authorities to effectively deal with crises involving cross-border insurance groups should be established. These arrangements could take the form of crisis management groups (CMGs) as currently exist for global systemically important insurers (G-SIIs).

A fundamental aspect of the Opinion refers to the scope of application. EIOPA considers that a harmonised recovery and resolution framework should cover all (re)insurers subject to the Solvency II framework. However, the application should consider the proportionality principle. In summary, EIOPA proposes to go beyond the current Financial Stability Board (FSB) entities-based approach of designating global systemically important insurers (G-SIIs) and to also cover other type of insurers.

A related and very relevant topic is the insurance guarantee schemes and resolution funding, which is a natural extension to EIOPA's approach on recovery and resolution.

In the European Union, there is currently a significant fragmentation regarding the existing schemes, which differ quite substantially in terms of financing, functions, mandate and coverage. This fragmentation creates particular problems in the presence of failures involving cross-border business and might result in a situation where policyholders in the European Union are treated differently, based on their residence and/or which insurer they contract with.

With the aim of triggering the discussion and collection the stakeholders' view, EIOPA recently published a "Discussion paper on Resolution Funding and National Insurance Guarantee Schemes" (EIOPA, 2018b), investigating the different sources of resolution funding as well as providing an overview of the existing national Insurance Guarantee Schemes and potential problems that may arise from the current fragmented landscape.

EIOPA is of the view that a minimum degree of harmonisation of the recovery and resolution framework in the European Union would benefit policyholders by enhancing consumer protection but also the insurance market and more broadly the financial stability in the European Union. How to achieve this required harmonisation is currently under discussion.

IV Systemic risk and macroprudential policy in insurance

The fact that the insurance sector may face severe distress and that the causes of such distress is a relevant microprudential concern is common sense. And it is not enough to raise macroprudential concerns only. Both the microprudential and the macroprudential perspective should be considered together as useful supplements.

EIOPA initiated a dedicated work stream with the aim of better understanding if and how insurance could create systemic risk. EIOPA took a sequential approach, seeking to answer the following fundamental questions:

- Does insurance potentially create or amplify systemic risk?
- If yes, what are the tools already available?
- Is there any need for additional tools and measures?

As shown in Figure 3, EIOPA considers that systemic risk in insurance can materialise in two ways (EIOPA, 2018c). Firstly, the 'direct' effect, originated by the failure of a systemically relevant insurer or the collective failure of several insurers generating a cascade effect, i.e. the 'entity-based' source. Secondly, the 'indirect' effect, in which possible externalities are enhanced by engaging in potentially systemically relevant activities (activity-based sources) or the widespread common reactions of insurers to exogenous shocks (behaviour-based source).

Defining the sources of systemic risk is the cornerstone of a macroprudential framework. Authorities responsible for the macroprudential policy should seek to mitigate these sources by means of relevant macroprudential tools (see Table 1).

In a first instance, however, the focus should be put on already existing measures and instruments, which contribute to mitigating the sources of systemic risk. Indeed, although Solvency II is in essence a microprudential framework, it contains relevant features that help mitigating the potential sources of systemic risk identified in insurance. For example, EIOPA (2018d) has shown that tools such as the symmetric adjustment in the equity risk module, the volatility adjustment, the matching adjustment, the extension of the recovery period or the transitional measure on technical provisions can contribute positively to limiting procyclicality.

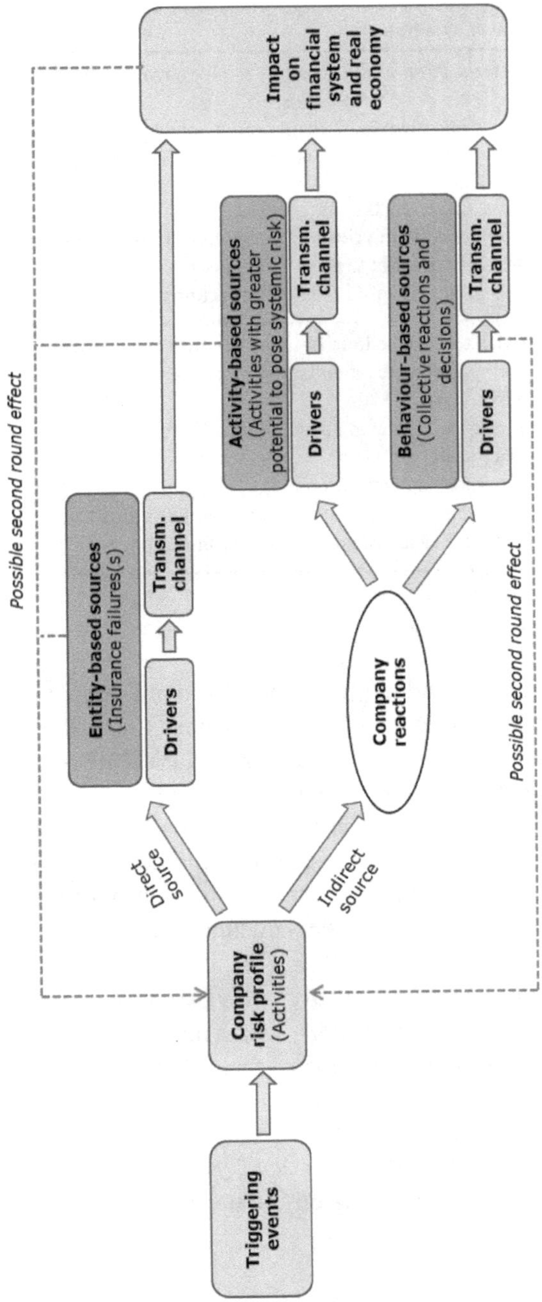

Figure 3: Insurance and systemic risk.
Source: EIOPA (2018c)

Table 1: Sources of systemic risk identified.

	Sources of systemic risk

Entity-based sources	– Deterioration of the solvency position leading to:
	  – Failure of a G-SII, D-SII
	  – Collective failures of non-systemically important institutions as a result of exposures to common shocks

Activity-based sources	– Involvement in certain activities or products with greater potential to pose systemic risk – Potentially dangerous interconnections
Behaviour-based sources	– Collective behaviour by insurers that may exacerbate market price movements (e.g. fire-sales or herding behaviour) – Excessive risk-taking by insurance companies (e.g. 'search for yield' and the 'too-big-too fail' problem) – Excessive concentrations – Inappropriate exposures on the liabilities side (e.g. as a result of competitive dynamics)

Source: EIOPA (2018c)

At this stage, EIOPA is further oconsidering possible additional tools and measures that could be included in light of the review of Solvency II in order to enhance the existing toolkit of authorities. For this purpose, EIOPA (2018e) carried out a preliminary analysis focusing on four categories of tools: a) Capital and reserving-based tools; b) Liquidity-based tools; c) Exposure-based tools; and d) Pre-emptive planning. EIOPA is also considering whether the tools should be used for enhanced reporting and monitoring or as intervention power. Following this preliminary analysis, EIOPA concludes the following (Table 2).

From the 15 tools and measures analysed by EIOPA, only two were deemed as not necessary. First, countercyclical capital buffers, which may work well in banking, but are not necessarily fit for purpose in insurance. Other alternatives (e.g. capital surcharges) are probably be better placed to address the potential risks. Secondly, liquidity requirements. While there seems to be a general agreement that monitoring liquidity at market-wide level is fundamental to avoid liquidity tensions, there is no clear evidence on the need to impose specific liquidy requirements yet.

Table 2: Additional tools and measures under consideration.

Tool	Type of tool	Proposed for further consideration?
Enhanced reporting and monitoring		
Leverage ratio	Capital and reserving-based	Yes
Enhanced monitoring against market-wide under-reserving	Capital and reserving-based	Yes
Additional reporting on liquidity risk	Liquidity-based	Yes
Liquidity risk ratios	Liquidity-based	Yes
Enhancement of Prudent Person Principle	Exposure-based	Yes
Enhancement of ORSA	Exposure-based	Yes
Recovery plans	Pre-emptive planning	Yes
Resolution plans	Pre-emptive planning	Yes
Liquidity Risk Management Plans	Pre-emptive planning	Yes
Systemic Risk Management Plan	Pre-emptive planning	Yes
Intervention powers		
Counter-cyclical capital buffer	Capital and reserving-based	No
Capital surcharge for systemic risk	Capital and reserving-based	Yes
Liquidity requirements	Liquidity-based	No
Temporary freeze on redemption rights	Liquidity-based	Yes
Concentration thresholds	Exposure-based	Yes

Source: EIOPA (2018e)

As a next step, EIOPA will continue further elaborating its views on the topic. The long-term objective is coming up with a formal proposal of additional tools and measures to be included in the context of the Solvency II review.

V Conclusions

There is a need for adequate policy responses to tackle the challenges ahead. These responses must, however, be tailored to the business model of insurers and the ways in which the sector may contribute to create or amplify systemic risk.

As described here, the resolution of insurance companies is not an exceptional occurrence when insurers are facing distress. Under certain instances, e.g. in case of failure of systemic insurers or where collective failures triggered by exposures to common shocks occur, the issue might even take a system-wide dimension.

EIOPA will continue to work focusing on both the microprudential and the macroprudential areas. In the medium-term, it is fundamental, both for consumer protection and financial stability reasons, to build a minimum harmonized approach to recovery and resolution and national insurance guarantee schemes on the microprudential side, as well as an effective framework to deal with the potential sources of systemic risk on the macroprudential side.

References

EUROPEAN COMMISION (2002): "Report on the prudential supervision of insurance undertakings" (Sharma Report), Conference of Insurance Supervisory Services of the Member States of the European Union, December 2002.

EIOPA (2017): "Opinion to Institutions of the European Union on the Harmonisation of Recovery and Resolution Frameworks for (Re)Insurers Across the Member States", 5 July 2017.

EIOPA (2018a): "Failures and near misses in insurance: Overview of the causes and early identification".

EIOPA (2018b): "Discussion paper on Resolution funding and national insurance guarantee schemes".

EIOPA (2018c): "Systemic risk and macroprudential policy in insurance".

EIOPA (2018d): "Solvency II tools with macroprudential impact".

EIOPA (2018e): "Other potential macroprudential tools and measures to enhance the current framework".

Giulio Terzariol

Resolution for insurers – no need to reinvent the wheel

The financial crisis in 2008 triggered an unprecedented level of legislative and regulatory activity on a global scale with the target to make the global financial system more resilient. Since then, a plethora of new regulations has been implemented across all sectors, with the International Association of Insurance Supervisors designating so-called Global Systemically Important Insurers (GSIIs), including Allianz, which are subject to additional regulatory requirements like recovery and resolution planning, liquidity and systemic risk planning as well as dedicated capital surcharges.

Nearly 10 years after the financial crisis and after most of the implementation work has been completed, it seems appropriate to take stock and review the progress made so far. This article focuses on the topic of resolution for insurers and provides perspectives from a European insurance industry point of view.

In 2014 the Financial Stability Board (FSB) published their "Key attributes of effective resolution regimes for financial institutions" with the goal to resolve an entity "without severe systemic disruption or exposing taxpayers to loss, while protecting vital economic functions through mechanisms that make it possible for shareholders and unsecured creditors to absorb losses in a manner that respects the hierarchy of claims in liquidation". A specific objective of the resolution regime for insurers was the protection of policyholders, beneficiaries and claimants. Key elements of effective resolution regimes were described as shown in the graphic below.

Note: I would like to thank Tobias Buecheler, Head of Regulatory Strategy, Group Regulatory Affairs & Public Policy for his invaluable assistance in preparing this article.

Giulio Terzariol, Chief Financial Officer, Allianz SE

https://doi.org/10.1515/9783110644067-008

Perspectives on resolution of financial institutions

Key elements of resolution regimes and and related tools*

Key elements	*Tools*
Effective cross-border co-operation	• Create legal framework • Institution - specific cooperation agreements • Crisis management groups
Resolution powers and tools	• Replace management • Control and operate firm • Transfer (of business) • Create bridge institutions / deposit guarantees • Order temporary stays
Total Loss Absorbing Capacity	• Additional loss absorbing capacity in resolution • Creditor bail - in ordered by authorities
Critical Functions	• Ensure operational continuity of vital functions
Resolution plans	• Advance Planning • Ensure resolvability

* Based on Key Attributes of effective resolution regimes by the Financial Stability Board

The Key Attributes require each jurisdiction to "have a designated administrative authority or authorities responsible for exercising the resolution powers over firms within the scope of the resolution regime ("resolution authority")". As such, resolution proceedings are under the remit of supervisors, with the industry having to support related requirements and planning in advance to ensure "resolvability" in line with the goals stated above.

When discussing resolution for insurance, it is worthwhile to keep in mind the origins of the debate stemming from the banking sector. In this context the clarification of key differences in business models between banks and insurers and their implications for relevant resolution approaches is important – one size fits all does certainly not apply for effective resolution.

As one can see from the next table: "resolution" is a much more critical issue for banks than for insurers from a timing as well as value at stake for policyholders and tax payers perspective: While banks might need to be resolved "over the weekend" to avoid a bank run with potentially systemic implications on Monday morning, insurers can be and have successfully been put into a multi-year run-off process where no additional capital is required and policyholders typically receive all or almost all of their benefits.

Characteristics of the business model relevant for effective resolution		
Criteria	**Banking**	**Insurance**
Time horizon of the business model	Short-term focus	Long-term perspective
Balance Sheet	Maturity transformation (short-term funding, long-term assets)	Largely asset-liability matching for balance sheet management
Relevant services	– Money creation – Operation of the payment system	Insurance services (risk consulting, claims management etc.)
Interconnectedness with financial system	High interconnectedness via interbank loan markets	Low interconnectedness between insurers and the wider financial system
Leverage	High leverage	Very low leverage
Profit sources	Income mainly derived from interest (differences) and trading	Income mainly from coverage of real risks and returns of long-term and high quality investments
Summary	Latent illiquidity resulting in "bank run" risk and need for short-term resolution	Pre-paid business model enabling long-term run-offs

If that is the case, why have insurers come into the focus of resolution regulation at all? Arguably, this was mainly triggered by the near failure of insurer AIG in 2008, which was ultimately prevented by the US government having provided a bail-out package totaling nearly 183 billion US Dollars. The demise of AIG was mainly driven by two operations (both of them not comprehensively supervised at the time):

- A substantial Credit Default Swap (CDS) short position portfolio (total notional 484 billion US dollars in 2008). When the financial crisis hit and credit worthiness of counterparties declined, this portfolio triggered consequently large margin calls. In this context it is noteworthy that especially CDS shorting is rather a trading strategy than an insurance activity – also illustrated by the fact that AIG's CDS portfolio made up 96% of the insurance sector's total CDS exposure at the time.
- A large Security Lending operation where the cash collateral received was invested into illiquid assets triggering a liquidity squeeze when the lending counterparties unwound the trades and called back their collateral. While Security Lending is also common for yield enhancement at many insurers,

the "doubling up" by investing cash collateral into illiquid, non-investment grade assets is again more trading than sound investment management – and also here the size was extraordinary with AIG making up 36% of the insurance sector's total exposure at the time.

Having these short-term trading type operations in mind, AIG does not seem to be well suited to serve as a justification for resolution requirements for the insurance sector in general.

In this context, it is also important to understand the prevailing supervisory framework for insurance. In Europe, Solvency II provides for a marked-to-market based framework for the whole balance sheet which requires insurers to hold sufficient own funds to withstand shocks which occur on average only once in 200 years. This requirement is complemented by a risk margin which is an additional buffer that – upfront – provides funds for the cost-of-capital of a third party taking over the insurer as part of an orderly run-off process.

As part of this framework and starting well before insolvency there is a clear "ladder of intervention" for supervisors which provides authorities early on with the tools needed to support an orderly run-off (instead of an unorderly failure), including the authority to require a pre-emptive recovery plan. Allianz as a Global Systemically Important Insurer has been required to develop pre-emptive recovery plans as part of systemic risk regulation since 2013. The recovery plan (together with further plans like liquidity risk management plans and systemic risk management plans) are submitted to the Group supervisor and further relevant supervisors who are members of the standing Crisis Management Group (which is a committee based on FSB recommendations to prepare for crisis response) annually. Allianz takes this crisis planning exercise very seriously and monitors so-called early warning crisis indicators on a monthly basis. The Group's recovery plan includes a detailed analysis of scenarios which could depress the solvency ratio towards the regulatory minimum, and describes related business, reputational and legal implications as well as mitigating recovery measures relevant for each scenario. For Allianz these plans comprise approximately 500 pages and are the result of a comprehensive process which includes all relevant internal stakeholders and takes several months to complete.

As such, pre-emptive recovery planning complements the existing risk management framework (which is focused on risk mitigation) with a different view (focused on recovery after extreme risk materialization), which – from our point of view – makes sense not only for GSII, but for the entire insurance industry.

Nevertheless, it is important to keep in mind that even if the Minimum Solvency Requirement of an insurer was breached, all insurance liabilities are typically still covered by high quality, largely duration matched assets so that usually neither policyholders nor tax payers face financial losses.

As a result, we believe that there is no need for additional capital in form of a "Total Loss Absorbing Capacity" like for banks – also because of the fact that European insurers usually do not issue substantial debt which could be bailed in (for Allianz only 8.6 billion Euro senior debt compared to a total balance sheet volume of nearly 700 billion Euro as of 2017). We therefore welcome the suspension of the related analysis by the IAIS (IAIS).

In addition, we are also rather reluctant regarding the concept of "critical functions" which have to be protected and kept operational during the resolution process. While the concept seems obvious for banks as operators of the payment system, it is far more elusive in insurance. In general, insurance markets are characterized by fierce competition and deep capacity for coverage. In addition, when looking at their relevance for the real economy it seems pretty muted. Even in somewhat concentrated markets like credit insurance – where Allianz for example has a global market share of approximately 26% – the premium volume (as a proxy for coverage) is below 1 ‰ of the GDP in literally all markets.

Our position is very clear: we believe that the most important elements for effective resolution of insurance companies are already in place and there is no need to develop new concepts which are alien to the insurance business model.

Does this mean that everything is fine for insurance and no further consideration is needed – obviously not. There are important lessons from the financial crisis which are relevant for the insurance sector as well:

- There is a clear need for group supervision which encompasses all entities within an insurance group – while Solvency II provides a strong framework for group supervision, this is still to be developed and fully implemented in some markets.
- The establishment of Crisis Management Groups is a powerful tool for effective exchange and discussion between international supervisors on all aspects of crisis management including recovery and resolution planning.
- Finally, in many countries authorities have key powers like suspending surrender rights for policyholders or enforcing portfolio transfers. These are important tools to ensure an orderly resolution which should be uniformly

developed across jurisdictions (the following graph shows the current status for selected EU markets):

Not all resolution tools exist in all jurisdictions…

Technical Debate Harmonization required	DE	F	I	AT	B	ES	IRL*	NL	PT	EU
Core resolution tools: Suspend policyholders' surrender rights	✓	✓	X	✓	X	✓	✓	✓	✓	X
Core resolution tools: Reduction of insurance obligations (bail-in)**	✓	✓	X	✓	X	X	✓	✓	X	X
Core resolution tools: Portfolio transfer	✓	X	X	✓	✓	✓	✓	✓	X	X
Recovery Planning***	✓	✓	✓	X	X	X	X	X	X	X
Restrict bonus + dividend payments	✓	✓	✓	✓	✓	✓	✓	✓	✓	✓
Replace senior management	✓	✓	✓	✓	✓	✓	✓	✓	✓	✓

* Answers relate to P&C business, only. Regulatory actions subject to Irish High Court approval
** Policyholders may not be better-off in liquidation
***As a precautionary measure, i.e. without breach of Solvency II capital requirements

…regulators need to ensure that they have effective stabilization tools at their disposal!

Last but not least I would like to turn to a somewhat different perspective and focus on the importance of management attitude and practice. While most stakeholders agree on the importance of pre-emptive crisis planning today, we must not develop a false sense of complacency based on progress achieved so far. As the next crisis might originate from a different place and unfold differently than the last, we need to continuously strive to improve our risk management practices to prepare for the unexpected – after all this is the raison d'etre of insurance. We owe this to our policyholders, shareholders and society as a whole.

Helmut Gründl

Some thoughts on recovery and resolution in insurance

In the past few years – after successfully introducing Solvency II, but also against the backdrop of potential distress scenarios associated with the current low interest environment – regulatory efforts in the European Union have increasingly focused on developing an effective and harmonized recovery and resolution framework for insurers.[1]

Regular insolvency proceedings designed for the overall economy do not specifically address policyholder protection and financial stability matters, and thus the continuity of critical functions[2] of insurance, especially in providing insurance coverage as a prerequisite for many risky economic activities or in providing life annuities, cannot be guaranteed.[3] Furthermore, in particular through the default of large insurers or the simultaneous default of smaller insurers, the infection of other parts of the financial system is possible.[4] In addition, liquidation is often time-consuming, possibly leading to several years' delay in settlement of claims filed and undermining the level of society's trust in the insurance sector.

Through early intervention, an effective recovery framework should provide a range of instruments to prevent distressed insurers from failing. However, if a failure becomes inevitable, effective resolution instruments have to be available to protect policyholders and preserve financial stability.

In the current low interest rate environment, insurers are increasingly likely to find themselves in financial difficulties.[5] However, as insurers' balance sheets gradually deteriorate, with an effective recovery and resolution framework in place, regulators and supervisors have time to adapt to various adverse scenarios.

---

1 See EIOPA (2017), ESRB (2017), FSB (2016).

2 According to ESRB (2017), critical functions are those "for which continuity should be maintained in the resolution process while avoiding unnecessary destruction of value".

3 See ESRB (2017).

4 See Kubitza and Gründl (2016).

5 See Berdin and Gründl (2015).

https://doi.org/10.1515/9783110644067-009

Recovery measures

In a recovery plan, a set of viable options is defined that an insurer could undertake in the event of financial problems.[6] Early development and maintenance of precautionary recovery plans can boost awareness of adverse events before they unfold. Insurers can assess their capabilities of withstanding a range of adverse developments and are better prepared to deal with possible recovery measures at an early stage. Generally speaking, financial stability and consumer protection can best be ensured when remedies for a situation can be found without the need for resolution as a last resort.[7] In the following, I will discuss some important recovery measures.

Asset/liability separation

By means of asset/liability separation, the regulatory authorities can reduce the burden on an insurer's balance sheet, while maintaining the continuity of critical functions. An asset/liability separation works in a way that a system is set up for separating liabilities and assets that allows the insurer's liabilities and related assets and rights to be transferred to a separate vehicle at a fair value.[8] The main objective is to separate non-performing combinations of insurance policies and assets held for them from viable combinations, and to transfer the non-performing asset and liability portfolios to a separate vehicle. However, it may be difficult to determine exactly which assets are being held for a subset of policies in the asset portfolio of the insurer. Applying the separation instrument to assets and liabilities includes disposing of them at fair value. Losses may be realized if there is insufficient time for the assets to return to their long-term economic value, inflicting losses on policyholders.

Surrender restrictions

Another important recovery tool – which can, of course, also be applied in a resolution context – imposes temporary limitations on the option of terminating insurance contracts. This measure affords the supervisory authorities

6 See ESRB (2017).
7 See FSB (2016).
8 See ESRB (2017).

additional time to focus on a distressed insurer. For example, the supervisory or resolution authority may choose to temporarily suspend the contractual termination rights of all parties so as to protect insurers and therefore lower the risk of unnecessary loss in value. This suspension is subject to ongoing performance of contractual obligations. This would avoid an impairment of the liquidity situation and market instability due to simultaneous termination of contracts by numerous policyholders. However, this tool is associated with some costs. Firstly, the application of this instrument in some EU member states could be confronted with enforcement issues under local law. Secondly, surrender limitations may well undermine trust and confidence in the insurance industry, and appropriate safeguards on its use should therefore be put in place. Thirdly, there is no certainty associated with the enforceability of surrender restrictions, in particular if the contract is subject to the law of a third party from a non-EU state.

Run-off

The run-off decision is initiated by the responsible regulatory authority and includes revoking the licence of an insurer to underwrite new business if a financial problem arises or in the event of non-compliance with Solvency II.[9] What justifies run-off as such is that while insurers may not be capable of expanding their business, they can still afford to meet contractual obligations arising from a current policy portfolio while being spared a great deal of the costs and disruption in connection with a normal liquidation.[10] In addition, the prevention on new business being transacted lowers an insurer's capital requirements and costs that new business entails. As a rule, however, run-off within the scope of resolution means that insurers can only meet their contractual obligations to a limited degree. A successful run-off also calls for policyholders to believe that their claims will indeed be paid. Otherwise, policyholders may terminate their policies, i.e., an insurance run may take place. In consequence, an insurer's asset portfolio may not contain adequate liquidity to cope with a flood of cancellations.

9 See ESRB (2017).

10 See ESRB (2017).

Portfolio transfer

In the case of a portfolio transfer, both the obligations to policyholders and the corresponding assets are transferred from a non-performing insurer to one or several third parties. Third-party providers include some other insurance company, a specialized run-off insurer, or a bridge institution.[11] Whereas portfolio transfers have been used both in the fields of banking and insurance, the processes certainly are not identical.[12] Unlike the situation in the banking sector, in which assets (i.e. loan portfolios) are swapped for other assets, in the insurance industry the portfolio transfer comprises both liabilities and the related assets in return for other assets.[13] A portfolio transfer therefore ensures the continuity of the insurance business, while the distressed insurer can be cut back without disruption as far as the transferred insurance contracts are concerned. It enables claims to be settled on time and reduces interruptions and the potential for the destruction of value. The main advantage associated with a portfolio transfer is that it is possible to maintain ongoing coverage for the insurer's business. However, a major challenge for portfolio transfers is the search for a willing buyer within an appropriate timeframe. The valuation of the assets and liabilities involved in a portfolio transfer may take time, and it may be necessary to set up a bridge institution. In addition, the process may be impeded by operational difficulties. A portfolio transfer might also be less practicable during systemic turmoil. The difficulty of locating a suitable buyer for a troubled insurer's business is intensified when the whole insurance sector faces a similar risk exposure.

Specialized run-off companies that serve as buyers of insurance companies and/or insurance portfolios, especially in the life area, have recently attracted a lot of attention. Run-off insurers such as Viridium are prepared to take over the portfolios of classical insurance policies and to continue the contracts until maturity. In July 2018 Generali announced the sale of 89.9 percent of the shares in its German subsidiary Generali Leben to Viridium. As a consequence, around four million life insurance contracts with guaranteed investments amounting to 37 billion Euros have come under the management of Viridium.[14] This makes the deal by far the largest transfer of a life insurance portfolio to a run-off company.

---

11 See ESRB (2017).
12 See ESRB (2017).
13 See EIOPA (2016).
14 See Viridium (2018).

In this context, the term "run-off" may have too negative connotations, being potentially associated with unwinding insurance contracts. A more appropriate description could go in the direction of "insurance portfolio management". It is also not clear to many policyholders that external run-off insurers are indeed genuine life insurance companies, the regulatory requirements of which are in no way less stringent than those of traditional life insurance companies. However, the culture of investors in run-off platforms, which are often private equity firms or hedge funds, can contribute to the culture of the company, and so it is quite conceivable that important attributes such as sustainability and customer loyalty may not be as pronounced in run-off insurance companies as in traditional life insurance. This may be particularly noticeable in the transition of contracts from mutual insurers.

However, the great advantage of run-off-company solutions can be the more efficient administration of existing contracts. In run-off companies, inefficient computer systems of the ceding companies, stemming from different decades, are merged and thus fixed costs can be reduced in the long run. However, in the current, still very early phase of external run-off – especially in Germany – the future development is not yet clear. The new run-off companies are presently working on the migration of the acquired life insurance portfolios. However, creating a unified IT standard is very costly and causes major operational risks. Presently, it is difficult to predict whether the benefits of external run-off solutions will outweigh the costs.

Although run-off insurers incur no costs for customer acquisition, marketing and advertising, there is the risk that only little attention will be paid to the needs of existing customers, as no new business is underwritten and thus no negative effects on future revenues need to be taken into account. In order to maximize profits, the run-off platform can theoretically minimize profit participation, especially through its accounting policy. However, it should be noted that even with such measures, higher surpluses are possible if a portfolio is in external run-off than would have been possible with the previous selling insurer.

Bail-In

Another potential recovery tool might be a bail-in arrangement, which could enable losses to be quickly allocated to and absorbed by shareholders and creditors. A bail-in entails techniques available to restructure liabilities or raise equity capital. This might be accomplished by restricting or writing off liabilities of debt providers or through the conversion of such liabilities into equity or equity-like instruments.[15] The bail-in instrument could therefore help to absorb losses and recapitalize the insurer. A tool of this kind would also ensure the ongoing prevalence of critical functions and might help to avoid systemic risks of the insurance sector.

Recovery instruments can be seen as a protective shell that not only protects policyholders, but may also protect unprofitable and inefficient insurance companies from market withdrawal. Unprofitable insurers could be kept artificially alive by recovery measures, and consumers would ultimately bear the costs of such market frictions, as they would possibly be exposed to more expensive products and inefficient claims handling. However, in the insurance sector, policyholders are to be protected against insolvency risks, especially in personal insurance. For this reason, "creative destruction" through both market entries and exits has to preserve policyholders' interests. These deliberations lead to the discussion of resolution measures.

Resolution measures

In case recovery and early intervention measures fail, specific resolution measures have been developed for insurers, especially since the financial crisis in 2008. Some of these are inspired by instruments in the banking sector. Let me shortly discuss some of these measures, with a focus on insurance guarantee schemes.

Liquidation

Liquidation is the usual procedure of insolvency proceedings and deprives the insurer of its authorization.[16] In the course of liquidation, all insurance policies are terminated, with current premiums being paid back to policyholders. All insurance claims are quantitatively recorded and evaluated. In addition, this involves resorting to corresponding insurance guarantee funds and, as a rule, all assets are sold. The insurer's assets are distributed among the various creditors in the order prescribed by law. However, liquidation cannot guarantee ongoing critical functions and is a rather time-consuming process. Lessons learnt in the financial crisis of 2008 indicate that the liquidation of a financial institution can lead to a substantial negative impact on the financial

15 See EIOPA (2017).
16 See EIOPA (2017).

system. The process can actually take a number of years, also involving instances of delay in settlement of outstanding claims, which may undermine public confidence in the insurance sector as a whole.[17] Therefore, solutions are needed that go beyond standard insolvency law and accelerate claims processing and payment so that policyholders are not disadvantaged but protected in the event of insolvency. Nevertheless, liquidation is a valid and useful instrument as part of an effective set of resolution tools, particularly for insurers lacking critical functions.

Bridge institutions

A bridge insurer takes over a failed insurer for a certain period and thus ensures that critical functions are maintained, including claims payments to policyholders. The bridge insurer is commissioned to continue the business of the insolvent insurer until such time as the portfolio has been assigned to a buyer.[18] This transaction offers potential buyers sufficient time to conduct the corresponding due diligence review of the failed insurer. A bridge insurer could particularly be beneficial in crisis situations in which there are only few willing buyers. It enables the liquidating authority to respond without delay by maintaining the insurer's value until its portfolio can be disposed of to a third party. The reason why policyholders stand to benefit is that a bridge institution guarantees the continuity of their coverage and payments. In this way, this instrument contributes to maintaining stability and confidence in the insurance industry. However, the creation of a bridge insurer also raises certain difficulties. Firstly, operating a bridge institution is work-intensive. Secondly, the financing of the bridge insurer must be clarified, in particular with respect to a possible recapitalization by a compensation fund or an insurance guarantee scheme. Furthermore, the search for a private purchaser may be difficult. If a sale to a private owner cannot be realized at an adequate price, then the bridge insurer's operating costs may exceed the costs of liquidation, which means that liquidation could be the better solution.[19]

17 See ESRB (2017).
18 See EIOPA (2017).
19 See ESRB (2017).

Insurance guarantee schemes

Insurance guarantee schemes and resolution funds are sector-financed resolution tools. The main task of a resolution fund is to finance all settlement actions carried out for an insolvent insurer, such as liquidation, and sale of companies.[20] In contrast, the insurance guarantee scheme has a primary function in settling policyholders' claims,[21] thus protecting policyholders if an insurer happens to fail.

As Solvency II cannot guarantee fail-safe conditions for insurers, insurance guarantee schemes have a further positive impact on the market by maintaining consumer confidence and minimizing market turmoil if an insurer happens to fail. Insurance guarantee schemes offer consumer protection as a last resort if insurers cannot meet their contractual obligations. In this way, they protect the insured in case their claims are not met if their insurer becomes insolvent. Yet the existence of an insurance guarantee scheme can also have potential negative impacts regarding the behavior of market participants (such as moral hazard). However, alternatives, e.g. as ex-post state intervention, might entail even more substantial disadvantages.[22]

Insurance guarantee schemes and resolution funds can be funded either ex-ante by means of regular contributions from insurers prior to an insurer's default, or ex-post by compensation processes after a default has occurred.[23] In a hybrid model the two approaches can be combined. In this case – as soon as an ex-ante fund has advanced to a targeted level – it is possible for contributions to be lowered or even cancelled altogether. One example to illustrate a hybrid approach is the "Protektor" insurance guarantee scheme for life insurers located in Germany, which is primarily financed ex ante, but also includes an ex-post feature.

Ex-ante financing offers various advantages but also entails a number of drawbacks. As regards liquidity, it supplies liquid funding to cover liquidity requirements in the initial phase of a default. As far as credibility is concerned, an insurance guarantee scheme or resolution fund is endowed with the resources necessary to shield policyholders and helps to finance the resolution process, particularly if no state guarantee is available. Furthermore, ex-ante financing may be considered to be fairer for the insurance sector as a whole as all companies bear the cost of insolvency, i.e. also the insolvent company. With regard to procyclicality, the build-up of ex-ante funds in good times allows a financial buffer to be

20 See ESRB (2017).

21 See EIOPA (2017).

22 See Dong/Gründl/Schlütter (2015).

23 See ESRB (2017).

created in order to cover failures of insurers. As a result, the surviving insurers are hardly or not at all additionally burdened, and the probability of further losses is reduced. This makes it easier to absorb and allocate insolvency costs. In combination with risk-sensitive contributions to the guarantee scheme, insurers that assume higher risk and are therefore exposed to a greater probability of default can be burdened ex ante by higher premiums. This engenders a fairer cost distribution and encourages insurers to act less riskily. Ex-ante funds may also generate investment returns which could be used to cover operating costs. Yet ex-ante resolution funds or insurance guarantee schemes may impose higher administrative and operational costs on their management, such as for collection of contributions or handling their investments.

There are some arguments in favor of ex-post financing, although this form of financing also involves risks to financial stability. First of all, it could ensure more efficient capital allocation. Since it involves no regular contributions, insurers could use such funds more efficiently within the scope of their business activities to generate income as well as maintain liquidity. Moreover, ex-post financing entails lower operating costs in "good times", which means that insurance guarantee schemes or resolution funds do not give rise to investment or administrative costs. Third, the cost of ex-post funding could be lower for the industry since only the funding actually needed would be charged. The drawbacks are mainly linked to timing difficulties, particularly the possible inability to raise necessary funds in "bad times", and the fact that contributions from surviving companies could give rise to a potential risk of infection owing to the additional burden imposed in "bad times".

Concluding remarks

Recovery and resolution plans can help to identify and protect critical functions of insurers and can help to detect possible infection channels for financial instability. To be sure, a harmonized recovery and resolution system is needed in the European Union. Otherwise, a patchwork of recovery and resolution frameworks at national levels can reinforce existing fragmentation and exacerbate cross-border infection. It is noteworthy that the EU insurance industry reflects a higher share of cross-border activities than the banking sector in relation to its total activity.[24] Moreover, a patchwork of national recovery and resolution schemes does not foster financial integration within Europe and may give rise

24 See Schoenmaker and Sass (2016).

to uncertainties for market players concerning the scope of insurance coverage as well as recovery and resolution instruments.

References

Berdin, E., & Gründl, H. (2015). The effects of a low interest rate environment on life insurers. The Geneva Papers on Risk and Insurance-Issues and Practice, 40(3), 385–415.

Dong, M., Gründl, H., & Schlütter, S. (2015). Is the Risk-based Mechanism Always Better? The Risk-shifting Behavior of Insurers under Different Insurance Guarantee Schemes. Journal of Insurance Issues, 38(1), 72–95.

EIPOA (2016), European Insurance and Occupational Pensions Authority, Discussion paper on potential harmonisation of recovery and resolution frameworks for insurers. EIOPA-CP-16/009. Frankfurt am Main.

EIOPA (2017), European Insurance and Occupational Pensions Authority, Opinion to institutions of the European Union on the harmonization of recovery and resolution frameworks for (re)insurers across the member states. EIOPA-BoS/17-148. Frankfurt am Main.

ESRB (2017). European Systemic Risk Board: Recovery and resolution for the EU insurance sector: a macroprudential perspective. Report by the ATC Expert Group on Insurance. Frankfurt am Main.

FSB (2016). Financial Stability Board: Developing effective resolution strategies and plans for systemically important insurers. Basel.

Kubitza, C., & Gründl, H. (2016). Systemic Risk and Late Resolution of Economic Shocks. ICIR Working Paper Series. Goethe-University Frankfurt.

Schoenmaker, D., & Sass, J. (2016). Cross-border insurance in Europe: Challenges for supervision. The Geneva Papers on Risk and Insurance-Issues and Practice, 41(3), 351–377.

Viridium (2018). Viridium Gruppe und Generali Deutschland unterzeichnen Kaufvertrag für Generali Leben und etablieren umfassende Partnerschaft. Available at: https://www.viridium-gruppe.com/de/presse/pressemitteilungen/artikel/viridium-gruppe-und-generali-deutschland-unterzeichnen-kaufvertrag-fuer-generali-leben-und-etabliere/ [Accessed 14 Sep. 2018].

III Cross-Border Issues

José Manuel Campa

Resolution in Europe: Pending cross-border issues

1 Introduction

The crisis has provided a new paradigm around resolution and how to ensure banks can fail. This paradigm, especially in Europe, has been built around two basic premises: banks should be able to fail without affecting financial stability and without imposing a burden on taxpayers or public funds. This approach reflects the need, after the financial crisis to recover market discipline and avoid the reputational impact on the system: banks have to be part of the solution, not part of the problem. These developments have been undoubtedly positive but they also pose new challenging tasks for regulators, the industry, and individual institutions.

Banks are subject to numerous regulatory and resolution frameworks. These regulations have been significantly enhanced after the financial crisis but are also highly complex. Banks, and resolution authorities, need to be able to implement their resolvability along the lines set in the regulation, and so as to obey the two premises indicated above. This requires a good thorough understanding of each institution and of the situations in which resolvability may need to take place. The experience on resolving institutions under this new framework so far has been limited, although positive. We need to assure that the system is ready to execute according to what is expected in the regulation.

I will focus my remarks in this article on three key issues that I believe remain to be improved so as to guarantee an adequate resolvability of financial institutions.

2 The need to consider the existence of different business models

Resolution is institution specific. Although some common issues certainly exist in the resolution of any entity, the specific aspects of how the resolved entity will regain solvency, will preserve continuity of critical functions and ensure

José Manuel Campa, Global Head of Regulatory Affairs, Banco Santander

https://doi.org/10.1515/9783110644067-010

operations going forward will differ for each institution. The TLAC term sheet published by the Financial Stability Board (FSB) sets the basics for establishing the resolution strategy of global systemic financial institutions. This term sheet recognizes the existence of different business models among banks and that resolvability has to be firm specific.

The resolution regulation has been framed around the concept of a resolution entity. The strategy for resolving an existing bank can differ depending on whether that bank involves one or several resolution entities in case of its resolution. These entities have to be well identified so as to be able to clearly assign losses among liability holders of the institutions and to implement emergency actions that preserve the adequate performance of any critical functions. The regulation is increasingly recognizing that there are several resolution strategies according to the existence of different business models and that strategies around a Single Point of Entry (SPE) or Multiple Points of Entry (MPE) in resolution should be feasible.

The transposition of the TLAC term sheet into national regulation has also reflected the existence of these multiple strategies. Jurisdictions have a strong interest in assuring financial stability around potential resolvability of entities operating in their jurisdictions. This has led national jurisdictions to encourage the establishment of appropriate structures so as to ensure the resolvability within their borders. In a global industry like banking, this implies that coordination among jurisdictions and a level playing field across borders need to be ensured. A remaining area of concern in the implementation of resolution regulation is the extent to which it may affect the level playing field across the industry.

The initial proposal in the European Union was to require all credit institutions to have resolvability plans and sufficient eligible liabilities to absorb losses in case of resolution based on a single regulation (the BRRD) for all credit institutions. These requirements are currently under review and may be adjusted so as to provide a certain flexibility and proportionality in their application to different institutions. Although proportionality most likely will apply to smaller institutions mainly operating in a single member state, care should be taken that it does not alter the nature of competition and affect the level playing field. Applying different rules to local institutions than to multinational banks may put barriers to the single market and also hinder the establishment of an effective banking union.

A related second area of concern is the extension of the resolvability requirements to emerging countries. The lack of applicability of these rules in these jurisdictions may again distort competition and a level playing field. The establishment of TLAC requirements for subsidiaries of G-SIBs that operate in these countries may impose an additional burden on their ability to compete in the local markets, particularly in the commercial and retail side of the business that continues to be local in most jurisdictions. The TLAC term sheet already provides an extended calendar of implementation for emerging countries. To the extent that countries opt for this longer calendar the same should also apply for subsidiaries of G-SIBs in these economies.

Compliance with these resolution requirements implies that the amount of eligible liabilities that would need to be issued by banks could be potentially very large. The existence of a broad investor base for these instruments is in question. This is already a challenge in developed markets such as Europe. As discussed above, the applicability of resolution requirements to all credit institutions in the EU makes the estimates of funding requirements in the coming years very high and questions are raised about the investor appetite for such a large volumes.

The scale of suitable investors for these type of liabilities may be even more limited for some emerging economies and might push banks to depend on foreign investors and/or issue these instruments in foreign currencies. This will have an impact on funding costs and currency risk that will also increase complexity for financial stability.

Furthermore, there should be a broader convergence between the regulation of prudential and resolution requirements. In particular, the presence of international banks in third countries with strong regulatory frameworks in place should not be penalized as it is currently in the prudential and resolution framework. In particular, Additional Tier 1 and Tier 2 capital instruments and minority interests issued by intermediate holding companies in third countries should be included in consolidated capital requirements when these intermediate holding companies are subject to prudential requirements as stringent as those applied to credit institutions of that third country and those requirements are deemed equivalent to EU regulation.

Therefore, cross border coordination is key. As I will discuss later, coordination among different jurisdictions is essential when it comes to execution of a resolution strategy. High coordination is also needed when establishing regulations so as to make sure that distortions to the efficient provision of banking services do not arise.

A related area of concern for coordination relates to the extension of some of the resolution related requirements beyond the home jurisdictions. The requirements in the BRRD in Europe for the inclusion of clauses in contracts written in a non-EEA law governed contract giving contractual recognition of bail-in powers of EU financial regulators can be very difficult to comply with in practice. Article 55 of the BRRD requires this clause to be included in a very broad range of contracts where it is unlikely to be possible for banks, despite their best efforts, to obtain the insertion of such clauses. The use of standard international documentation and rules, the practice of having no express choice of governing law of contracts, and the inability to impose unilateral changes to a contract because of the dominant bargaining position of non-customers (overseas counterparties and beneficiaries) in many trade finance transactions make it almost impossible for banks to add contractual bail-in terms to some types of trade finance liabilities.

3 The need for liquidity provision in resolution

Banks that enter resolution most likely will face liquidity constraints. There is the need to have a clear framework so that the provision of liquidity if needed does not constitute an impediment to successfully implement the resolution strategy. A clear message needs to be sent following a resolution process that the bank is solvent again and that access to liquidity sources will mitigate concerns and facilitate private investors to step in.

The FSB has issued a proposal which aims at operationalizing funding within the resolution planning. A key principle that should operate is to ensure that the temporary funding needs of the firm in resolution are met to maintain the continuity of critical functions and ensure financial stability. To the extent market access to funding is not available or sufficient, credible public sector backstop mechanisms should be in place. Any use of these mechanisms should be rules based and subject to strict conditions so as to minimize the risk of moral hazard.

In Europe, the framework is still incomplete on this point. We need a clear backstop in case of funding needs and a credible liquidity backstop that allows the implementation of resolution plans. It also has to give confidence in the stages previous to resolution if needed, decreasing the risk that a solvent entity enters into resolution due to liquidity issues before even implementing measures included in its recovery plan and before the supervisory authority is able to consider early intervention measures.

This framework should also include protocols or ex ante agreements among host and home supervisors. In emergency situations, ring-fencing measures imposed by the host tend to be the usual response. Where coordination is required between authorities in respect of temporary public sector backstop funding mechanisms, the home resolution authority should consider establishing protocols with the relevant authorities to coordinate the provision of temporary backstop funding. Such protocols could set out the information sharing arrangements, notification requirements and key decision making considerations between the relevant authorities.

The bail-in process and the stabilization of the bank, through adequate management and a credible business plan so as to provide comfort to existing creditors could take not hours but days. A clear message needs to be sent following a resolution process that the bank is solvent again, able to continue its critical operations, and that access to liquidity sources will be provided. This will help mitigate concerns and facilitate private investors stepping in. This process may often require more than just one or two days.

Moratorium tools should never be applied before a bank is determined to be failing or likely to fail. Practical experience shows that the imposition of a moratorium leads to a massive loss of confidence in the stability of a bank and is usually a step towards insolvency. Early moratorium tools would increase the risk of an ultimate bank failure instead of stabilizing a troubled bank. Additionally, measures such as Emergency Liquidity Assistance cannot remain at national level and should be part of the coordinated liquidity toolkit around resolution.

The creation of the Banking Union has built institutions and regulations that put us in a much better position to guarantee that moral hazard, in the case of need for public support, will not arise (more and bigger capital and liquidity buffers, contributions to the deposit guarantee and single resolution Funds; issuance bailinable debt; recovery and resolution plans; and the elimination of barriers to resolvability). Therefore, progress along that route should be more feasible if deemed necessary.

4 The need for trust in execution

Resolution can only achieve its goal of maintaining financial stability if it is effectively executed. Resolution of an entity is always bad news and comes with a cost, but the system has to be ready to face it. Authorities have the responsibility to develop resolution plans and also to implement them in case the bank reaches the point of non-viability. However, bank managers also have a responsibility in operating their institutions so as to make them resolvable and to guarantee the continuity of their operations even under stress conditions.

The resolution framework is still being developed in many jurisdictions. Some jurisdictions have well established resolution institutions with a long tradition in liquidating and resolving banks (for instance the FDIC in the U.S.). However, this is the exception. In most jurisdictions across the globe resolution regulation is relatively new. The regulations are being approved, and in many cases new resolution authorities are being created with newly defined mandates. It is not easy to perform laboratory tests to assess how effective these regimes will be in resolving institutions. Unfortunately, the system will be tested as individual cases get resolved.

In the European Union the experience is very limited, and almost nonexistent in the case of the Banking Union. It is good news to see, through the resolution of Banco Popular last year, that the European framework proved to be effective and it was possible to resolve a financial entity without the use of public funds nor even the resolution fund. But one good experience should not lead to complacency

In emergency situations, all stakeholders tend to become more risk averse. Communication and coordination are as essential as a well-designed resolution strategy. As stated above, when the resolution involves an international bank, host authorities may have the intent to impose ring-fencing measures as a way to minimize the impact of the resolution in their jurisdiction. Therefore, global resolution can only work where there is coordination. Authorities need to plan ahead and make strong efforts to assure that they set the basis for that coordination to function smoothly when the need to resolve an institution arises.

Ex ante coordination leads to trust. This trust can prove extremely useful in the tense moments around a resolution. Coordination becomes key independently of the resolution strategy. In order to regain the confidence in the affected institution additional measures to reduce uncertainty are also needed: adequate valuation analysis; clarity on the quantity and type of instruments available to absorb losses and on the amount of loss attributed to each instrument; and a viable plan for the institution post resolution. A strong and coordinated communication strategy on all these issues by all stakeholders has also to be put in place.

Communication is an essential element. Coordinated communication is key to preserve the credibility of the process. A credible resolution framework is key for financial stability and market certainty. A coherent communication becomes more important when the number of regulators involved is large so as to avoid cacophony on the process or confusion on the different roles and responsibilities of everyone engaged in the process.

Lack of coordination or communication will lead to uncertainty on the outcome. The implementation of any resolution strategy will result in likely losses to some liability holders. Prior management will also likely disagree with parts of the diagnosis or the proposed action plans going forward. Challenge of the resolution plan from some of these stakeholders and litigation will likely follow. Markets and litigators can seize on inconsistent messages or differences of view among authorities to argue that less onerous alternatives could have been pursued with less damage to stakeholders; or that the process was not properly run. This will increase the uncertainty about the final outcome, delay the process, and increase the overall cost of resolution. A well coordinated and communicated resolution strategy is essential to minimize all these risks.

Wilson Ervin

Jurisdictional trust vs the 'Prisoner's Dilemma'... and plotting an escape from the prison

Europe has come a long way in making resolution practical across the EU. A sensible legal and policy framework has been adopted; the Bank Resolution and Recovery Directive (BRRD) and key institutions are now in place. Indeed the Single Resolution Board (SRB) successfully executed its first live transaction last summer (Banco Popular). However, a single swallow does not a summer make. To understand the current state of play, let's first review the key requirements for effective resolution:

1) High speed execution with clear legal powers
   a) Pre-planning can help (living wills)
   b) How do jurisdictions interact/ cooperate? (MPE vs. SPE*)
2) Protect critical economic functions
   a) Ideally these would be very senior
3) Preserve value / avoid fire sales
   a) Swap protocol and stays (some concerns over EU moratorium proposals)
   b) Sufficient emergency liquidity
4) Large supply of subordinated resources
   a) Total Loss Absorbing Capacity (TLAC) >20% Risk Weighted Assets (RWA)
   b) Market crediblity and clear expectations – avoid structural surprises
   c) Appropriate investors (avoid other banks, unsophisticated retail)

---

*Multiple Point of Entry vs Single Point of Entry resolution strategies

Figure 1: Key elements for effective bank resolution.

There is much good news across these categories for large banks in Europe. A number of big banks are resolvable now, and progress continues for the others. Figures 2 and 3 below provide a perspective on resourcing (point #4). TLAC

Wilson Ervin, Vice Chairman Global Executive Office, Credit Suisse

https://doi.org/10.1515/9783110644067-011

resourcing (also called MREL[1] in Europe) is already beyond FSB requirements in many countries (USA, UK, Switzerland, Germany), but there is work to do for other EU GSIBs. (G-SIB is the term used by the Financial Stability Board (FSB) for the largest banks (Global Systemically Important Banks).

However, some other important challenges remain for banks in many parts of Europe:

- Under regulatory leadership, the International Swap Dealers Assocation (ISDA) and the large trading banks agreed an ISDA OTC Protocol a few years ago. This agreement effectively averts the risk of an expencive and dangerous mass unwind. However, the EU is currently debating some idiosyncratic 'moratorium tools'; some of these are ill-designed and could upset that achievement (3a).
- We would also highlight structural concerns on 3b (sufficient liquidity). The ECB has constitutional constraints with respect to 'lender-of-last-resort' financing powers, and the Single Resolution Fund (SRF) is undersized for a major crisis. (In 2008, liquidity demands were on the order of trillions, while the SRF is targetted for a final size of approximately E 55 billion.) The ECB has begun to engage on this recently, and I would particularly commend President Draghi's May speech on the topic.
- Challenges also remain on 1b (cross border) – a focus of our later discussion.

Figures 2 and 3 below summarize the progress in resolution resourcing, and try to put this in a broader perspective. Many countries have issued ample amounts of effective, fully subordinated TLAC to support effective resolution. The U.S. situation is shown on Figure #2; while the European development of TLAC is at an earlier stage, the ultimate relationships should be similarly compelling. We are putting *massive* resources in place to deal with future crises.

A cross-border perspective for TLAC is shown above in Figure #3. The big question is: 'how much TLAC is enough for a successful resolution?'. For context, the most severe top-to-bottom drawdown of capital in the Crisis for *any* G-SIB scale entity was about 9% of RWA.[2] TLAC resources of 20% will allow a bank to experience a worst-case Crisis drawdown and still emerge with a strong, double digit capital ratio post-resolution. This TLAC needs to be properly subordinated

1 MREL means "Minimum Requirement for own funds and Eligible Liabilities". It consists of equity plus other (mostly subordinated) resources that can be bailed in to finance resolution.

2 This calculation is conservative as it ignores tax benefits from losses and any capital raising actions.

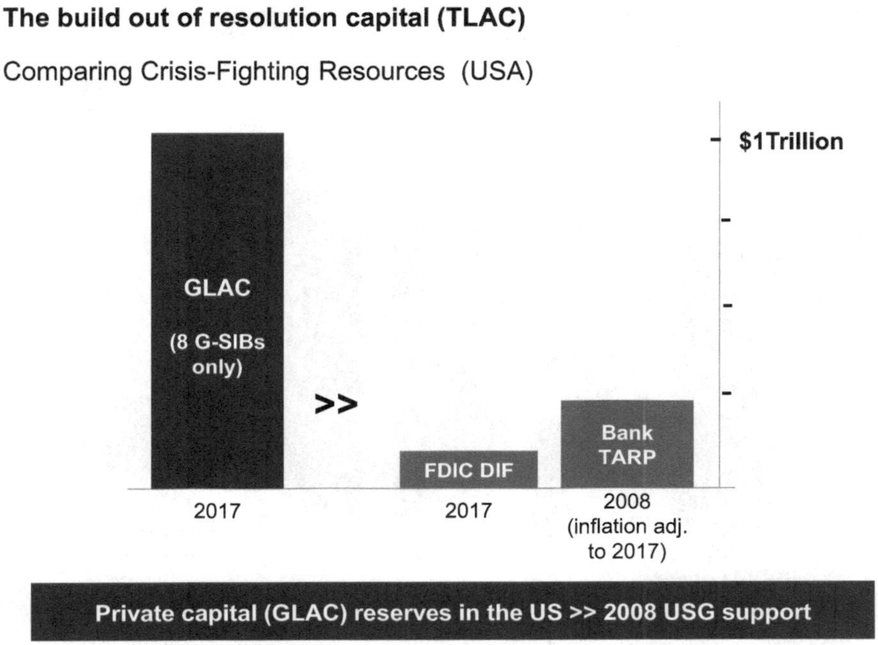

Figure 2: Resolution Resourcing (USA view).

and effective.[3] But if it satisfies those tests, a TLAC level of over 20% provides ample fuel to drive the resolution car where it needs to go.

Cross border cooperation

Let's turn now to cross-border cooperation, where significant policy development is still needed. While good laws and ample resources are perhaps the most critical elements for credible resolution, cross-border cooperation is also important. Some frame this as a 'trust' issue, but it's better to see this as a question of incentives and system design. How do we create a system that accepts

3 For example some banks in southern Europe sold bail-in securities to unsophisticated, local retail investors. When it came time to write down or convert these instruments (to provide fresh capital in resolution), there was a political outcry. In some cases, politicians decided to reimburse retail investors for the bail-in haircut. This frustrates the purpose of TLAC to provide resolution funding without State Aid.

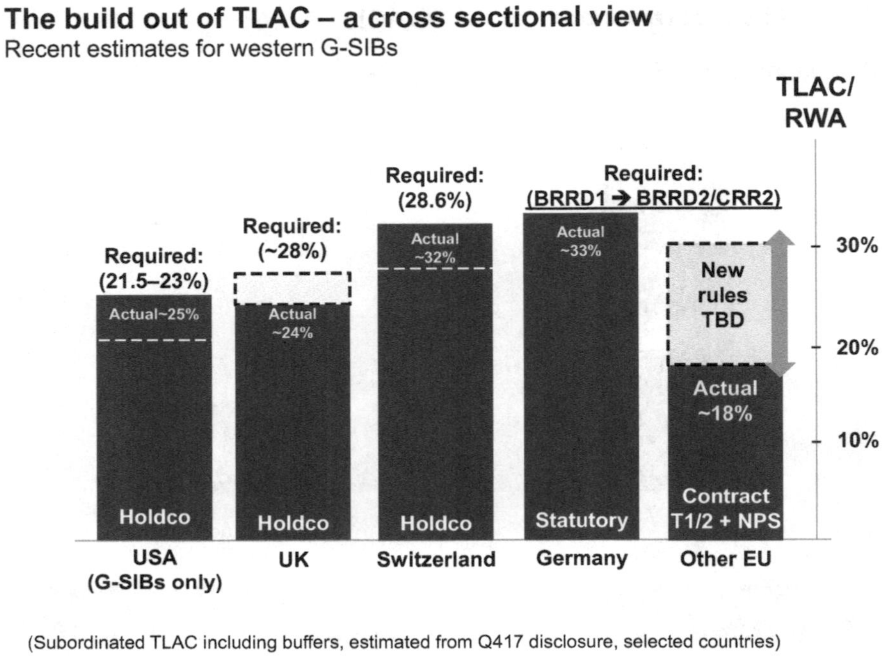

Figure 3: Resolution Resourcing (Cross border view).

national self-interest as a reality, and build rules to support cooperation across borders – and that will work under stressful, crisis conditions.

In recent years, jurisdictions have turned to ring-fencing as a way to protect themselves without needing to rely on the cooperation of others. (e.g. the US Intermediate Holding Company requirement (IHC), the EU Intermediate Parent Undertaking (IPU), and many others – both public and implicit). Indeed, current trends suggest that we are drifting toward a regime of 'endemic' ring-fencing, where local supervisors trap capital (and liquidity) extensively, and little flexibility remains at the group.

Ring fencing has 'curb appeal' for host regulators. It provides a straightforward tool to establish strong local control. However, it has major costs in terms of systems, governance and especially in treasury functions. Local control of key resources like equity, TLAC and liquidity seems attractive – but taken too far, it can impair bank safety.

Let's consider the size of these effects. In a working paper published a few months ago, we examined how a model bank would perform under different rign fencing structures, and how that would affect the likelihood of failure.

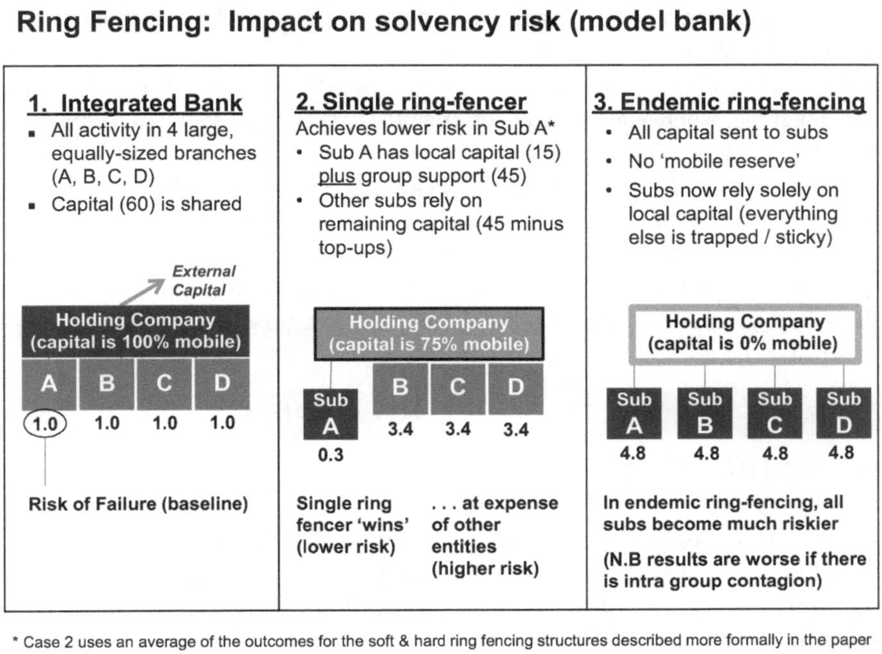

Figure 4: Ring Fencing: Impact on solvency risk (model bank).

Figure 4 shows how endemic ring-fencing can arise, and how far it can raise firm risks. It starts with a theoretical 'Integrated Bank' in the left box. In this case, capital is flexible, and can move to any entity that needs it.[4] Each entity shares the risk of the firm evenly, and we designate this risk level as 1.0. In the next (middle) box, a single ring-fencer decides to improve his or her position by trapping a proportion of capital, while still benefiting from the overall pool of capital at the group level if needed. In this case the ring-fencer has cut risk by 70% (to 0.3x), but the other entities see their risk rise dramatically (because some of the central reserve has been allocated elsewhere). If the next jurisdiction responds and ring-fence its own share of capital, then that jurisdiction does better – but the others are even worse off. If everyone follows their self-interest, and traps capital fully (the right hand box), then the central reserve will disappear. Each subsidiary is now on its own. Our model estimates the resulting solvency risk for the fully-ring-fenced bank is roughly *5x the integrated bank.*

4 For example, a bank built with branches inside a single legal jurisdiction could approximate such an entity.

Endemic ring-fencing means that assets are effectively boxed into local units, and each part of the bank becomes less diverse and riskier. Ultimately all jurisdictions end up worse off – even the first ring-fencer. This is a sort of 'prisoner's dilemma', where each jurisdiction tried to improve their individual situation, but the collective result was that everybody was worse off.

This right hand box – endemic ring-fencing and higher bank risk – is clearly a poor policy outcome! If jurisdictions (whether trans-Atlantic or intra-EU) adopt full ring-fencing, then bank failure risk can rise by a large multiple. And this result can get even worse – if the failure of one subsidiary leads to the failures of others in the group becasue of contagion, the risk of failure can rise by more than the figures shown here.

Some intuition

One way to understand this issue is that ring-fencing causes a problem called 'misallocation risk. This is the risk that the group has enough capital *overall* – but cannot move it to a troubled subsidiary in time. See Figure #5 below for a schematic that illustrates this concept.

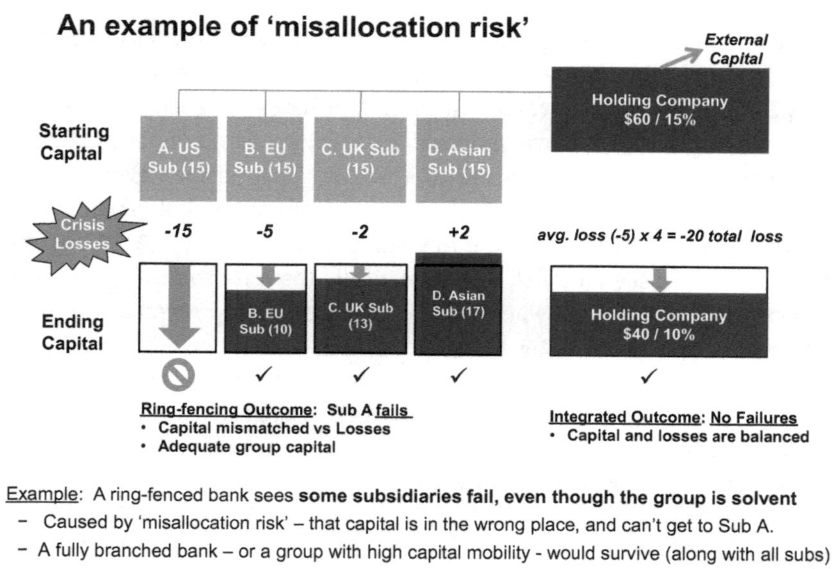

Figure 5: An example of 'misallocation risk'.

Summary

In my view, the home-host challenge is one of the 2 big issues remaining in the European resolution project. (Liquidity is the other.)

We need solutions that address endemic ring-fencing and create a more resilient system. Our suggestion is to use a predictable, transparent regime, and to set rules that limit preplacement to a moderate level.[5] The initial preplacement would be augmented by contractual arrangments (perhaps similar to the Secured Support Agreemements (SSAs) used in US Living WIlls). This package would encourage and incentivize cooperation while avoiding misallocation risk.

This system would acknowledge that home countries need a degree of 'certainty' and preplaced resourcing, while ensuring that we don't drift all the way to endemic ring-fencing. Home jurisdictions need to ensure sufficient flexibility to avoid misallocation risk that can drive up the risk of failure. A solution with these attributes could help repair the trust gap that has emerged between home and host jurisdictions. It would shift the challenge of cooperation from 'trust' to the firmer ground of well-designed local incentives, careful resourcing and legal requirements.

5 Our Working Paper "The Risky Business of Ring-Fencing" provides more detail around our solvency analysis, and also around our proposed solution. See: https://papers.ssrn.com/sol3/papers.cfm?abstract_id=3085649.

Mark E. Van Der Weide

An American perspective on the cross-border issues in large bank resolution

Introduction

The Federal Reserve has been a strong supporter of the core global bank regulatory reforms conceived and adopted by the Basel Committee on Banking Supervision (BCBS), the Financial Stability Board (FSB), and national jurisdictions since the crisis. These reforms have made the largest global banks substantially less likely to fail. The Federal Reserve also has strongly supported the international efforts to promote the orderly resolution of the largest global banks. These resolution efforts have reduced the damage that would be done to the financial system in the event of the failure or material distress of a systemically important bank.

Global and U.S. regulators have made substantial progress since the crisis in improving the prospects for an orderly resolution of a global systemically important bank (GSIB). The core areas of progress include adoption and implementation of new statutory resolution frameworks in major jurisdictions, development of the single-point-of-entry (SPOE) bail-in recapitalization resolution strategy, adoption by the FSB and national jurisdictions of total loss absorbing capacity (TLAC) requirements for GSIBs, adoption and implementation of resolution planning requirements, the crafting of solutions to the problem of early termination of qualified financial contracts (QFCs), and increased international coordination efforts.

Large bank failures are inherently messy, so it is impossible to fully specify the path of a bank's failure and the path of a failed bank's resolution. That said, one of the most useful aspects of the evolution of resolution science since the crisis has been the general gravitation of banks and resolution authorities toward the SPOE bail-in recapitalization strategy. This resolution model has not yet been tested in a real-life collapse of a systemically important bank, but it offers the prospects for a formidable simplification of the process around resolving a failed systemic bank. An SPOE resolution should be simpler for the home country resolution authority to conduct, simpler for a host country

Note: This article contains my personal views, which may not reflect those of the Federal Reserve Board.

Mark E. Van Der Weide, Federal Reserve Board

https://doi.org/10.1515/9783110644067-012

supervision authority to understand and trust, simpler for counterparties and the markets to predict outcomes, and simpler for the public to understand.

The resiliency and resolvability efforts of the global regulatory community have been predominantly focused on building up buffers in, strengthening home country supervision of, and enacting robust home country resolution frameworks for, the consolidated global banks. A material part of these efforts, however, has included enhancements to the resiliency and resolvability of the material operations that a global bank conducts outside its home country. This secondary objective is critical in my view because a necessary condition to the orderly resolution of a large bank with significant cross-border operations is instilling confidence in the local supervisors, creditors, and counterparties of the firm's foreign operations.

The resolution of a failed cross-border banking firm is doomed to disorderliness in the absence of excellent regulatory cooperation among home and host supervisors. Statutory resolution frameworks in the home country of a GSIB generally only apply to legal entities that are chartered in the home state of the firm. Foreign subsidiaries and foreign bank branches of a GSIB could be ring-fenced or wound down separately under the insolvency laws of their host countries if foreign authorities do not have full confidence that local interests will be protected. Accordingly, the successful resolution of a large, cross-border banking firm will require that home-country authorities provide credible assurances to host-country supervisors to prevent disruptive forms of ring-fencing of the host-country operations of a failed firm. The ultimate strength of these arrangements will depend on whether they have adequately addressed the shared objectives, as well as the self-interests, of the respective home and host authorities. The groundwork for these arrangements is being laid now.

I will cover, architecturally, two topics in this article. First, how the Federal Reserve as host supervisor has worked to improve the resiliency and resolvability of the U.S. operations of foreign banking organizations (FBOs). Second, how the Federal Reserve as home supervisor has worked to ensure that the cross-border operations of our U.S. GSIBs do not impede their resolvability.

The Federal Reserve as host supervisor

Let me start with the Federal Reserve as host. The Federal Reserve introduced a set of enhanced prudential standards for the U.S. operations of foreign banks in 2014 in response to substantial increases in the size and risk profile of foreign banks in the United States in the decade and a half before the crisis and in response to the substantial contributions of foreign banks to the strains in the U.S. financial markets in 2007–09.

The Federal Reserve pursued a number of goals in its foreign bank enhanced prudential standards – including simplifying the structure of the U.S. operations of FBOs, getting more local capital and liquidity in the U.S. operations of FBOs, improving the resolvability of the U.S. operations of an FBO if the FBO were to fail, and right-sizing the future liquidity that FBOs might require from the Federal Reserve.

Our core FBO reforms have included four key elements. First, we have required foreign banks with at least $50 billion in assets in U.S. subsidiaries to place their U.S. subsidiaries under a U.S. intermediate holding company (IHC). Second, we have required U.S. IHCs of FBOs generally to meet the same capital requirements as similarly sized U.S. BHCs. Third, we have required foreign banks with at least $50 billion in U.S. assets (subsidiaries plus branches) to keep a liquidity buffer in their U.S. operations. Fourth, we have imposed internal TLAC requirements on the U.S. IHCs of foreign GSIBs to better enable U.S. authorities to cooperate effectively in a global resolution of the foreign bank.

These reforms have resulted in a meaningful restructuring of the largest U.S. operations of foreign banks and meaningful enhancements to their resiliency and resolvability. We have attempted to strike the right balance between permitting foreign banks to flexibly allocate resources inside the global firm and requiring foreign banks to locally pre-position loss absorbency and liquidity resources in the United States. Our attempt to tailor our FBO IHC proposal to strike the right balance is reflected in a number of dimensions of our current regime, including: (i) we only require FBOs to estabish an IHC if they have more than $50 billion of assets in U.S. subsidiaries; (ii) we continue to permit FBOs to operate in the United States through direct branches and agencies with no local capital and no local TLAC; (iii) we have not required FBO IHCs to implement the advanced approaches risk-based capital requirements; and (iv) we have not imposed GSIB capital surcharges on U.S. IHCs of foreign GSIBs. Of the roughly two hundred foreign banks that have U.S. banking operations, only twelve are required to establish IHCs in the United States and only nine of these twelve are required to meet internal TLAC requirements.

The Federal Reserve continues to believe that the FBO IHC framework is appropriate for foreign banks with large U.S. operations. As with all regulatory frameworks, however, we will be open to considering adjustments that would preserve the resiliency and resolvability benefits of the framework but improve its transparency, efficiency, and simplicity. The Board's Vice Chairman for Supervision has recently indicated his view that the Board should consider a few potential adjustments to our TLAC regime, including our calibration of internal TLAC requirements for IHCs.

The Federal Reserve as home supervisor

The Federal Reserve also has addressed cross-border resolution issues as a home supervisor of our eight GSIBs, most of which have very substantial footprints outside the United States and particularly in Europe.

Our efforts in this field have included adoption of a muscular set of external TLAC requirements for U.S. GSIBs. The U.S. version of external TLAC requirements is consistent with the FSB standard but stronger in a number of respects. The U.S. regime, for example, contains a separate long-term debt (LTD) requirement, a higher calibration of various minimum requirements and buffers, and a tighter definition of what counts as eligible LTD.

In addition, the Federal Reserve, working jointly with the Federal Deposit Insurance Corporation (FDIC), has developed a Resolution Capital Adequacy and Positioning (RCAP) framework for the U.S. GSIBs. The Federal Reserve and the FDIC employ the RCAP framework to help ensure that the U.S. GSIBs (i) have the capability to measure the stand-alone loss absorbency needs of each of their material subsidiaries; and (ii) allocate appropriate amounts of going and gone concern loss absorbency to their material subsidiaries around the world. The RCAP framework is a relatively flexible internal-stress-test based regime that recognizes the tradeoffs between pre-positioning to comfort local supervisors and local counterparties and retention of contributable resources at the parent holding company to reduce misallocation risk.

The Federal Reserve also endeavors to help ensure that the U.S. GSIBs have an adequate distribution of liquidity throughout the firm to ensure their resiliency and resolvability. SPOE bail-in recapitalization is designed to maximize the prospects that the material operating subsidiaries of a failed GSIB will be quickly recapitalized to a strong level so that they are able to fund themselves in the private markets during the resolution. If market confidence does not return quickly enough for private market funding to suffice, however, we can maximize the prospects for an orderly resolution if the failed GSIB has appropriately distributed liquidity throughout the firm in advance and has retained sufficient supplemental liquidity at its parent holding company. Our goal is for host country authorities to be assured that their local interests will be protected without ring-fencing.

Our first line of defense in this regard is the Liquidity Coverage Ratio (LCR). The global application of the LCR, although not designed as a resolvability reform, helps produce an appropriate distribution of liquidity throughout a global banking firm. For each U.S. GSIB, for example, we subject the consolidated global firm to the LCR, and we subject its U.S. subsidiary banks to the LCR on a sub-consolidated basis. The United Kingdom and other major jurisdictions impose the LCR on the major foreign subsidiaries of each U.S. GSIB. Moreover, the LCR is structured so that the global consolidated LCR of a banking firm suffers if the firm has trapped excess liquidity in regulated subsidiaries. All of these features of the worldwide LCR contribute to the appropriate distribution of HQLA throughout the firm.

The LCR is a powerful liquidity distributive tool, but it does not help ensure, for example, that there is enough HQLA in (or available to) the U.S. non-bank subsidiaries or the material foreign branches of a U.S. GSIB. To supplement the work of the LCR, the Federal Reserve and the FDIC developed a Resolution Liquidity Adequacy and Positioning (RLAP) framework for the U.S. GSIBs. Under this framework, the Federal Reserve and the FDIC help ensure that U.S. GSIBs have the capability to measure the stand-alone liquidity position of each material entity in the group and maintain appropriate amounts of liquidity either pre-positioned in material entities or available for easy transfer to material entities. Material entities include material subsidiaries (foreign and domestic) of the GSIB and material foreign branches of the GSIB's subsidiary banks. Like RCAP, RLAP involves each GSIB making internal-stress-test based estimates of liquidity needs and liquidity resources and recognizes the need to strike the right balance between full pre-positioning of HQLA inside each material entity and retention of an HQLA buffer at the parent holding company for flexible deployment throughout the firm as needed in stress.

Another critical way in which the Federal Reserve has helped to move the ball forward on cross-border resolution is our support for efforts to address the problem of early termination of QFCs. We have supported efforts by the private sector to address this problem though an industry protocol, and we have issued our own rule to make sure that QFCs entered into by U.S. GSIBs under foreign law would be subject to appropriate contractual stays that prevent their disorderly unwind in the resolution of the firm.

Conclusion

One of the most salient lessons learned from the financial crisis was the need for an orderly resolution regime for systemically important banking firms. The global regulatory community has made impressive progress on this front over the past decade. One of the key remaining issues for policymakers in this field is to find the appropriate balance for GSIBs between the ex ante pre-positioning of resources in material operating units of the group and the retention of contributable resources at central command for tactical allocation ex post to the group's material operating units in times of stress. I look forward to continuing work on this critical issue, in partnership with our international central bank, supervisory, and resolution authority colleagues.

Thomas F. Huertas

Resolution: Ready to go?

Ending too-big-to-fail is one of the cornerstones of post-crisis regulatory reform. Ten years after the great financial crisis, where do we stand? If a major bank were to reach the point of non-viability, are the authorities ready to resolve it?

The answer depends largely on whether authorities are able and willing to cooperate with one another. At the behest of regulators and supervisors, banks are making themselves resolvable. Investors are on notice that they will be at risk if a bank fails, and rating agencies now expect bail-in to be the norm, not bail out. So whether too-big-to-fail ends is now largely up to the authorities. They have the responsibility to form, communicate and execute the resolution plan, not the bank.[1]

Here, further progress is needed. Although authorities have mapped out two alternatives (the single point of entry [SPE] and multiple point of entry [MPE]), these alternatives depend upon cooperation among the authorities, both within jurisdictions and across jurisdictions.

This is a frail foundation for resolution. Resolution regimes do not necessarily promote cooperation. Within jurisdictions, the central bank generally lacks a formal seat at the table in determining the initiation and execution of the resolution plan, even though its decision with respect to emergency liquidity assistance (ELA) largely determines when resolution will be triggered, and its decision with respect to liquidity provision to the recapitalised bank-in-resolution largely determines whether resolution will succeed or fail.

With respect to cooperation across jurisdictions, authorities face a dilemma. They are aware that cooperation will yield the best global solution, but they recognise that cooperation may not yield the best result for their own jurisdiction or be consistent with their own mandates. Indeed, resolution regimes generally instruct authorities to frame their decisions with respect to financial stability within their own jurisdiction rather than global financial stability. Hence, each authority must assume that other authorities will put their own interest first.

1 In the United States, banking groups have to submit plans for how they would resolve themselves under the bankruptcy code, but the bankruptcy code does not apply to the bank subsidiary. Nor can the banking group develop a plan under Title II of the Dodd-Frank Act. Such plans are the responsibility of the FDIC as resolution authority in consultation with other US authorities.

https://doi.org/10.1515/9783110644067-013

That in turn has prompted two responses. First, authorities are talking with one another, in so-called crisis management groups, about how they could cooperate to resolve each globally significant bank (G-SIB). But their deliberations largely concern the processes they should employ rather than the decisions they should reach. Moreover, the conclusions of these groups are not binding on the participating authorities. Second, authorities are taking steps to reduce the need for cooperation. These steps are diminishing the effectiveness and efficiency of global banks without necessarily enhancing their resolvability. Instead, authorities should take steps to foster cooperation as well as co-opt the market into promoting such cooperation, both within and across jurisdictions.

Too-big-to-fail is too costly to continue

The failure of a major bank is a major event. If such a bank ceases to operate, millions of households and businesses may be unable – at least for a time – to access their accounts, to make or receive payments, or to buy and sell securities. The failure of a major bank can therefore create a ripple effect, first on the bank's customers and counterparties, then possibly on financial markets and the economy at large.

In 2008 that ripple effect was a tsunami. The failure of Lehmans caused financial markets to collapse and that in turn threw the world economy into reverse. That economists now speak of 2008/9 as the Great Recession rather than the Greater Depression is due to the timely provision of emergency assistance to financial institutions and markets as well as to the immediate injection of monetary and fiscal stimulus by central banks and governments around the world.[2]

Although rescuing the banks saved the economy, policymakers quickly concluded that too-big-to-fail was too costly to continue. It destroyed the public finances, distorted competition and incentivised banks to take excessive risks. G-20 leaders therefore mandated officials to devise a way to end the need for governments to bail out banks,[3] to make the ripple effect from bank failure akin to that produced by a pebble plopping into a pond. That would be the case, if

2 There is an extensive literature on the causes and consequences of the crisis. For the latest view see (Tooze 2018). For a critical summary of early assessments see (Lo 2012). For my own view see (Huertas 2011a).

3 (G-20 2009).

the bank-in-resolution could continue its critical economic functions without having to turn to the taxpayer for solvency support.

The global solution: Resolution as "pre-pack" bankruptcy

"Bail-in, not bail out" is the collective solution developed by policymakers under the aegis of the Financial Stability Board. This amounts to a special regulatory procedure on a global scale akin to a "pre-pack" bankruptcy. It envisions the immediate recapitalisation of a failed bank by investors, not taxpayers, so that the failed bank can reopen promptly for business as usual on the first business day following its placement into resolution.

Practically all the elements for this solution are now in place. Jurisdictions have implemented the key attributes for effective resolution regimes, as recommended by the Financial Stability Board.[4] They have enacted requisite legislation, created resolution authorities and endowed them with appropriate powers and resources. Specifically, legislation and regulation has defined the point at which the authorities may put a bank into resolution, the creditor hierarchy (including the preference for deposits) that the resolution authority has to respect, and the stay that authorities may impose on investors invoking their rights to terminate qualified financial contracts such as repos and derivatives.

In addition, regulators have mandated banks to take steps to make themselves resolvable.[5] These include a requirement that banks maintain a minimum total loss-absorbing capacity ("TLAC") well in excess of their current common equity Tier I capital requirements.[6] If the bank reaches the point of non-viability, this excess should be sufficient to recapitalise the bank as well as restore market confidence in the bank. A significant portion of TLAC must therefore be issued in the form of "gone-concern capital," eligible for bail-in (write-down or conversion into common equity). Banks must disclose to investors in such "gone-concern capital" the risk that they could be bailed in as well as take the measures necessary to ensure that the bank could issue enough

4 (FSB 2014a) lists the key attributes. (FSB 2017a, 26–29) documents compliance with key attributes by major jurisdictions.
5 G-SIBs are subject to an annual resolvability assessment process (FSB 2016b, 12). For guidelines on how supervisors should conduct such assessments see (EBA 2014); (BoE 2015).
6 (FSB 2015a) details TLAC requirements and provides term sheet for qualifying instruments. Regarding the FSB's plans to monitor the implementation of this standard see (FSB 2018a).

new common shares to accommodate any conversion.[7] These arrangements create the basis for investors, not tax-payers, to recapitalise the failed bank.

Banks also have to ensure that they can continue to operate, even whilst they are in resolution.[8] Banks must frame contracts with affiliates and third-party providers so that the bank-in-resolution continues to receive the services it requires. Together with financial market infrastructures (FMIs) banks must make arrangements to ensure that the bank-in-resolution retains access to FMIs so that it can clear and settle transactions once it reopens for business.[9] Banks have to able to furnish to the resolution authorities up-to-the-minute information concerning their assets and liabilities, including the degree to which assets are encumbered and/or eligible for discount under normal central bank facilities.[10] Finally, authorities may order the bank to remove any structural impediments to resolvability, such as complex forms of organisation, a high degree of inter-affiliate funding or offering overly complex products.[11]

All this effort has created the basis for authorities to end too big to fail. Indeed, rating agencies now proceed under the assumption that authorities will bail in rather than bail out investors, especially in instruments, such as Additional Tier 1 capital, Tier 2 capital and senior non-preferred debt that count toward TLAC requirements.[12]

To make the "pre-pack" work authorities must cooperate with one another

Cooperation is needed at each stage of the resolution process: at its inception, when the authorities pull the trigger and place the troubled bank into resolution; during the stabilisation phase on the "resolution weekend," when the authorities recapitalise the bank via bail-in; and during the restructuring phase, in particular when the bank reopens for business on the "Monday" following the resolution weekend as well as during the process whereby control over the bank-in-resolution passes back from the resolution authority to the new owners of the bank. This cooperation needs to occur both within and across jurisdictions.

7 See (FSB 2018b) for details.
8 (FSB 2016a).
9 (FSB 2017b).
10 (FSB 2017c).
11 See for example (EBA 2014).
12 (Moody's Investor Services 2014).

Cooperation within jurisdictions: The role of the central bank

To illustrate the need for cooperation within jurisdictions, we take the case where the bank is organised as a single legal vehicle (the bank itself) and where the bank has no foreign branches. Such a bank has to interact with a number of authorities: its regulator, its supervisor, the central bank, the deposit guarantee scheme and the securities regulator. In addition, the bank interacts with financial market infrastructures and indirectly with the regulators and supervisors of such infrastructures.

Cooperation among these authorities is necessary at the inception of resolution to ensure that resolution gets off to the right start. A bank should be placed into resolution as soon as it reaches the point of non-viability. Indeed, the entire resolution "architecture" is based on the premise that the authorities will not engage in forbearance; that the authorities will intervene in a timely manner at a point where the troubled bank still has positive net worth. That helps ensure that TLAC instruments will be sufficient to recapitalise the bank.[13]

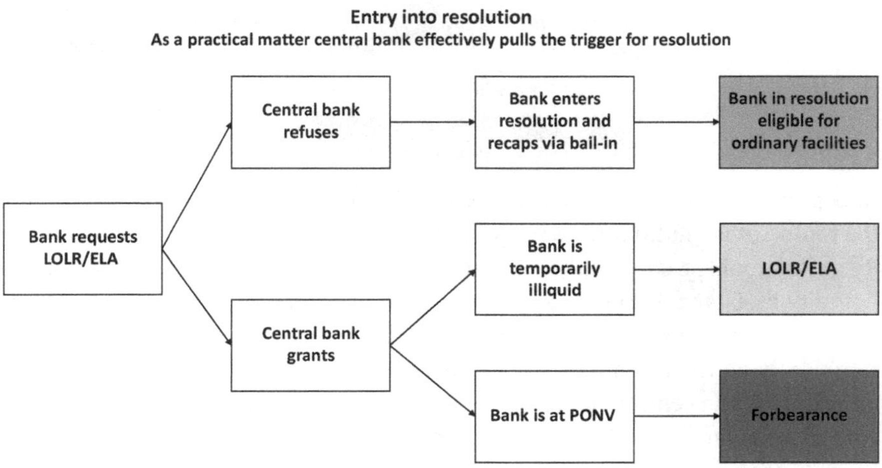

However, resolution regimes largely ignore the key role of the central bank. For example, in the EU the BRRD takes steps to ensure cooperation between the

13 The recapitalisation amount is based on the assumption that intervention occurs at the point where the failing bank's net worth is positive but close to zero, so that the recapitalisation amount must be sufficient to enable the bank-in-resolution to meet all current capital requirements. In addition, the resolution authority may set an additional market confidence charge. See (FSB 2014b); (FSB 2015b); (FRB 2015) (Deutsche Bundesbank 2016).

resolution authority and the supervisor (competent authority), but fails to consider the role of the central bank. The supervisor (competent authority) has the primary responsibility for determining whether the bank is "likely to fail,"[14] and the resolution authority has the responsibility to determine whether

> having regard to timing and other relevant circumstances, there is no reasonable prospect that any alternative private sector measures … would prevent the failure of the institution within a reasonable timeframe.[15]

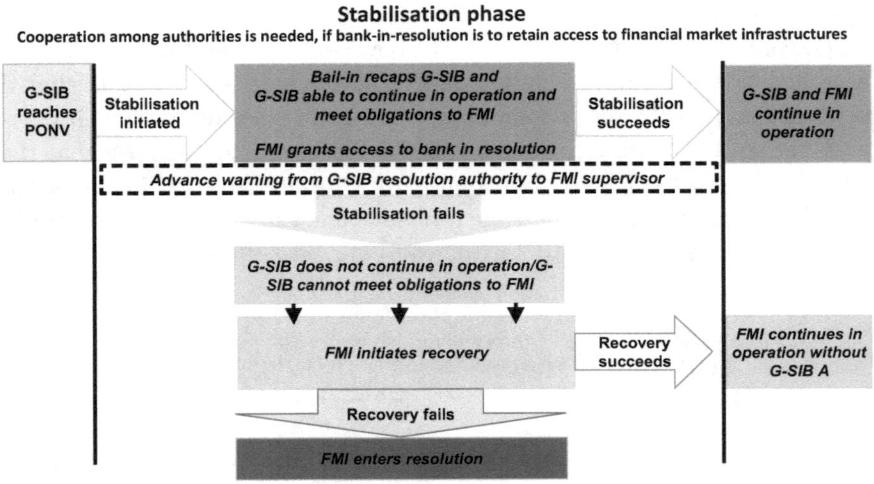

As a practical matter, however, it is generally the central bank that determines the timing of resolution. As long as the central bank is willing to provide liquidity to the troubled bank (either through normal liquidity facilities or emergency liquidity assistance), the bank may continue in operation. This may allow private creditors to reduce their exposure to the troubled bank and losses at the troubled bank to accumulate. If left unchecked, forbearance may occur (i.e. liquidity from the central bank allows the troubled bank to continue in operation with insufficient capital). That in turn may induce management of the troubled bank to "gamble for resurrection," further aggravating losses. By the time resolution is initiated, the bank may have significantly negative net worth. If so, its TLAC instruments may be insufficient to recapitalise the bank, and resolution will be more difficult, if not impossible.[16]

---

14 BRRD Art. 32 (1)(a).

15 BRRD Art. 32 (1)(b). The resolution authority also has the responsibility to determine whether resolution measures would be in the public interest [BRRD Art. 32 (1)(c)].

16 For further discussion see (Huertas 2018).

During the stabilisation phase cooperation between the resolution authority and supervisors needs to be close. This pertains not only to cooperation between the resolution authority and supervisor of the bank in resolution, but also between the resolution authority for the bank-in-resolution and the supervisors of the financial market infrastructures in which the bank-in-resolution is a member. The resolution authority will need to ensure that the bank-in-resolution maintains access to the FMIs in which the bank is a member on the basis that the recapitalisation will enable the bank in resolution to continue to fulfil its obligations to the FMI (see Figure). In particular, measures should be taken to ensure that the CCPs do not allow the entry of the bank into resolution to trigger immediately the close out of the bank's positions, the initiation of the default waterfall and the liquidation of any collateral posted by the bank-in-resolution.[17]

Cooperation among the authorities is also essential during the restructuring phase. Once recapitalised via the bail-in process at the "weekend," the bank-in-resolution will re-open on the "Monday". However, it will only be able to stay open (and therefore continue to perform its critical economic functions), if it has access to adequate liquidity. This should include access to normal central bank lending facilities against eligible collateral under standard conditions.

Yet in some jurisdictions central banks are reluctant to state in advance that they would allow the bank-in-resolution to have such access. They do not wish to fetter their discretion. They believe ambiguity is constructive.

In this case, it is not. When the bank-in-resolution reopens on the "Monday," it has been recapitalised via bail-in. It is solvent and meets minimum capital requirements. It is under the control and direction of the resolution authority. It should therefore have access to normal central bank lending facilities on normal conditions.[18] Any doubt that this will be the case is likely to cause the resolution plan to fail.

Rather than run such a risk, authorities should take steps to ensure that the central bank is involved in its role as liquidity provider in the creation of the resolution plan and committed to its successful implementation.[19] The central

---

17 Huertas (2016a).

18 To implement this decision, the authorities need to ensure that the central bank can immediately take charge of the collateral that the bank-in-resolution would need to pledge to the central bank. In particular, the central bank needs to be able to take over the collateral that the bank-in-resolution had pledged to repo lenders.

19 Even in cases where the central bank is the supervisor, the provision of liquidity, especially emergency liquidity assistance, may be decided separately from supervision. A case in point is the SSM. The ECB takes supervisory decisions in the Single Supervisory Board, but national central banks make decisions regarding liquidity support.

bank should determine during the stabilisation phase on the "resolution weekend" whether the bank-in-resolution will meet the standards for access to normal liquidity facilities so that the degree of bail-in may be adjusted, if necessary. Waiting until the "Monday" to do so would be counterproductive. The time for ambiguity is before, not after, the bank enters resolution.

Finally, the resolution authority and the supervisor will need to cooperate during the restructuring phase. Although the resolution authority controls the bank-in-resolution, the bank is not and should not be exempt from supervision. The resolution authority will need to keep the supervisor informed of its plans for the bank so that the supervisors may provide its approval in a timely fashion. This is especially important in the days following the re-opening of the bank (when the resolution authority may initiate sales of subsidiaries and/or lines of business) as well as in connection with the "exit" from resolution via the return of control to the owners of the bank.

Cooperation across jurisdictions

When a bank operates in multiple jurisdictions, its resolution involves interaction among home and host authorities. Will they cooperate or act independently, if the bank enters resolution?[20] Although crisis management groups have discussed cooperation extensively, the words used in such forums don't speak as loudly as authorities' actions to fragment global banks and thus remove the need for cooperation.

Crisis management groups are developing joint resolution plans for globally significant banks. In line with the recommendations of the FSB,[21] authorities have formed a crisis management group for each of the thirty globally significant banks (G-SIBs). These groups consist of the supervisory authorities, central banks, resolution authorities, finance ministries and the public authorities responsible for guarantee schemes of jurisdictions that are home or host to entities of the group that are material to its resolution. They meet periodically among themselves to develop and refine the resolution plan for the G-SIBconcerned, as well as with the G-SIB itself to review its condition, assess its recovery plan and communicate to the G-SIB a joint supervisory

20 For an overview of the issues involved see (FSB 2015b).

21 According to the FSB Key Attributes (FSB 2014a), "home and key host authorities of all G-SIFIs should maintain CMGs with the objective of enhancing preparedness for, and facilitating the management and resolution of, a cross-border financial crisis affecting the firm".

programme, including any instructions to the G-SIB on how it should improve its resolvability.

In most cases, the authorities have concluded bank-specific Cooperation Agreements detailing the objectives of resolution and how the home and host authorities would interact with one another to achieve these objectives, if the bank were to enter resolution.[22] However, the Cooperation Agreements stop short of establishing a presumptive path that the authorities would attempt to follow, if the bank reached the point of non-viability. The Agreements are non-binding and focus on the processes that the authorities will follow, for example, with respect to the sharing of information, rather than the decisions that the authorities will have to reach.[23]

Restricting the agreements to process poses a significant risk. Any cooperation agreed within the CMG in "peacetime," need not indicate how the authorities would react, if the G-SIB in question were to reach the point of non-viability and require resolution. There is little time on the "resolution weekend" to negotiate cooperation, especially in light of the complex processes that each authority has to follow within its own jurisdiction and the priority that authorities have to accord to domestic concerns. Thus, CMG statements provide only limited guidance to investors on the loss that they could incur, if the bank were to enter resolution.

Structural reform reduces, but does not eliminate, the need for cooperation. In addition to exploring how they might cooperate with one another, authorities are also seeking ways to reduce the need to cooperate with one another. To enhance resolvability, authorities have required banks to align legal vehicles and business units. In addition, authorities are imposing restrictions on the transactions that subsidiaries may conduct with one another. These include limits on lending to affiliates. This facilitates separability, namely the ability to sell a line of business by selling the stock of the legal vehicle conducting it, or the ability to put that legal vehicle into resolution whilst treating the rest of the group separately.[24]

In part, these measures stem from a belief that structure supports safety. In a number of jurisdictions (e.g. United Kingdom, Switzerland) authorities have

22 (FSB 2014a).

23 (FSB 2011b) lists the essential elements of cooperation agreements. See (EBA 2017) for an example of such a cooperation agreement.

24 For example under the BRRD Art. 17 (5)(g) the resolution authority may require changes to the legal or operational structures of the institution so as to reduce complexity to ensure that critical functions may be legally and economically separated from other functions through the application of the resolution tools.

taken steps to separate domestic retail and commercial banking from purportedly riskier foreign and/or investment banking activities. In other jurisdictions (e.g. United States) host-country authorities have required foreign banking organisations to place all their subsidiaries into a single intermediate holding company (IHCs) subject to the same prudential and supervisory standards applicable to "domestic" banking groups (i.e. groups headquartered in the host country).[25]

Host countries generally seek to insulate such IHCs from the failure of the parent, as well as to put in place procedures that will induce or force the parent to act as a source of strength to the IHC and its subsidiaries in the host country. Host countries generally require the foreign parent of the IHC to "pre-position" TLAC within the host country as well as to remove any obstacles to the host country's ability to force the IHC to write down or convert "gone-concern capital" into common equity Tier I capital prior to the entry into resolution of the bank itself or its affiliates in the home or other host countries.[26] Such a power to force the parent to top up the capital of the subsidiary in the host country whilst that entity has significant positive net worth effectively takes away the banking group's option to walk away from such an entity.

Open issues. Neither discussions in crisis management groups nor actions to atomise banking groups create certainty among investors as to how resolution would proceed and what recovery, if any, they might achieve, if the bank on whom they held a claim were to enter resolution.[27] This uncertainty increases the risk and potentially the cost of TLAC instruments, such as Tier 2 capital (subordinated debt) and senior non-preferred debt.

As outlined above, the principle source of uncertainty is the timing of the failing bank's entry into resolution. In addition to the possibility that the central bank will foster forbearance, there is a very practical issue of determining whether the home or the host country authorities will place the bank into resolution. To illustrate this, take the case where the troubled bank is a single legal vehicle operating in two jurisdictions. It has its headquarters in its "home"

25 For further discussion see Huertas (2016b).

26 See for example (FRB 2017, 8270). If the parent holding company declines to put in such additional resources, it runs the risk that the host-country authority will initiate the resolution of the subsidiary and sell the entity to a third party for less than the book value of the subsidiary. Rather than incur such a loss, the banking group will generally find it preferable to inject the additional capital demanded and then sell the subsidiary itself.

27 Nor does "no creditor worse off" protection offer much comfort. Its point of comparison is the loss that the creditor would incur under immediate liquidation of the bank's assets at fire-sale prices. Under such circumstances it is unlikely that holders of TLAC instruments would realise any recovery at all.

country and a branch in its "host" country. The business day closes in the home country whilst the host country is still open. What happens if the bank cannot meet its obligations at the close of business in the host country? Should it be entirely up to the host country's central bank to decide whether or not to provide the bank's branch with sufficient liquidity to meet its immediate obligations? If so, that is tantamount to giving the host country's central bank the power to "pull the trigger". If the host country central bank does not agree to provide the necessary liquidity, the bank will default on its obligations and the bank will fail. Note that this is the case for every global bank headquartered outside the Western Hemisphere that has a branch in the United States. In effect, the Federal Reserve has the option to put any such bank into resolution that cannot meet its obligations in dollars to US financial market infrastructures and other creditors at the close of the US business day.

Further uncertainty arises, during the stabilisation phase, if the host country authorities have the option to liquidate the branch of the bank-in-resolution located within their jurisdiction separately from the rest of the bank. This would effectively scupper the home country's resolution plan for the bank. The home country authorities would potentially be forced to liquidate rather than resolve the bank. That would make it impossible for the bank-in-resolution to continue to perform its critical economic functions, with adverse consequences for financial stability in the home country and possibly beyond. These concerns applies to practically every global bank headquartered outside the United States. Each of these banks has a branch in the United States, and the United States implements international insolvency proceedings according to the territorial principle. In this case, the host country would liquidate the branch as if it were a subsidiary. The assets booked in the branch would be used, first to satisfy the obligations of the branch. Any net proceeds remaining after the conclusion of the branch liquidation process would be transferred to the home country to the estate of the failed bank.[28] Hence, resolution plans for non-US global banks depend critically on the cooperation of the United States. To date, there is no guarantee that such cooperation will be forthcoming.

Cooperation between home and host authorities is also needed in the case of banking groups. Take the case where the banking group consists of a parent holding company headquartered in the "home" country. This entity owns two banks, one headquartered in the home country and another in the host country. Neither bank has branches outside the country in which it is incorporated and neither bank has exposure to the other. For the home country, the question is

28 (Lee 2014).

the degree to which the host country will follow the lead of the home country. If the home country bank fails, and the home country authorities place the home country bank as well as the parent holding company into resolution, will the host country authorities allow the parent holding company to continue to control the group's bank in the host country (i.e. to follow a single point of entry approach)? Or will the host country authorities place the host country bank into the host country's resolution process independently of the home country? If so, are there safeguards against the host country resolution authority selling the group's bank in the host country to a third party without the consent of the parent holding company or the home country resolution authority?

The case for a presumptive path

In sum, much has been done to reform resolution and to make banks resolvable so that banks are "safe to fail". Authorities have put in place the framework to enable the bank-in-resolution to continue to perform its critical economic functions whilst investors, not taxpayers, bear the cost of failure. Banks have taken steps to make themselves resolvable, including issuing the significant amounts of the "gone-concern" capital necessary to recapitalise (via bail-in) the bank-in-resolution.

Nonetheless, there remains the risk – despite all the planning and preparation for resolution – that resolution reform will fail to achieve its objectives. Specifically, there remains a risk that the cooperation that occurs in a carefully constructed and coolly conducted simulation will evaporate in the hectic and heat of an actual crisis.

Rather than run this risk, authorities should do three things. First, they should make sure that central banks have a full seat at the resolution table and that resolution plans fully encompass the role that central banks play in determining the initiation of resolution and the ability of the bank-in-resolution to obtain liquidity when it reopens on the "Monday" following the resolution weekend. And, the central bank should make clear that upon reopening the recapitalised bank-in-resolution will have access to normal central bank liquidity facilities.

Second, jurisdictions should recognise, if necessary by amending relevant legislation and/or regulation, that promoting financial stability globally is consistent with enhancing financial stability domestically. This would remove instructions to the authorities to focus on domestic concerns only and create the basis for authorities to cooperate with one another across jurisdictions.

Third, for each G-SIB its crisis management group should disclose to the market the presumptive path that it would intend to pursue, should the G-SIB or one of its material resolution entities reach the point of non-viability. Although this path would not be binding on any of the authorities and would be subject to change at the point at which the authorities initiated resolution, the path's publication would provide details on how the authorities plan to handle the open issues outlined above, especially the timing of resolution, the provision of liquidity to the bank-in-resolution and the exit of the bank from resolution. Moreover, the path's publication would lay bare the extent to which authorities intend to cooperate with one another as well as express their commitment to do so.

For investors, such publication would have two effects. It would confirm that they are at risk, if the bank enters resolution. But it would also help investors estimate loss given resolution for each class of obligation in the creditor hierarchy. This in turn would enhance market discipline and reinforce the effectiveness of resolution regimes. In other words, it would help make banks "safe to fail".

References

BoE 2015. Bank of England. "The Bank of England's power to direct institutions to address impediments to resolvability." Accessed 30 August 2018. https://www.bankofengland.co.uk/-/media/boe/files/financial-stability/resolution/boes-power-to-direct-institutions-to-address-impediments-to-resolvability-statement-of-policy.pdf?la=en&hash=F13D4A38B380D8206E245AB9EA1DC4950F6489AE.

BRRD 2014. European Union. "Directive 2014/59/EU of the European Parliament and of the Council of 15 May 2014 establishing a framework for the recovery and resolution of credit institutions and investment firms and amending Council Directive 82/891/EEC, and Directives 2001/24/EC, 20." Accessed August 25, 2014. http://eur-lex.europa.eu/legal-content/EN/TXT/?uri=CELEX:32014L0059.

Deutsche Bundesbank. 2016. "Bank recovery and resolution – the new TLAC and MREL minimum requirements." *Monthly Report*. Accessed 30 August 2018. https://www.bundesbank.de/Redaktion/EN/Downloads/Publications/Monthly_Report_Articles/2016/2016_07_minimum_requirements_tlac_mrel.pdf?__blob=publicationFile.

EBA 2014. European Banking Authority. "Guidelines on the specification of measures to reduce or remove impediments to resolvability and the circumstances in which each measure may be applied under Directive 2014/59/EU." 19 December. Accessed August 30, 2018. https://www.eba.europa.eu/documents/10180/933988/EBA-GL-2014-11+%28Guidelines+on+Impediments+to+Resolvability%29.pdf.

EBA 2017. European Banking Authority. "Framework Cooperation Arrangement." September. Accessed August 30, 2018. https://www.eba.europa.eu/documents/10180/1762986/Framework+Agreement+-+EBA-US+agencies+-+September+2017.pdf.

FRB 2015. Board of Governors of the Federal Reserve System. "TLAC."
FRB 2017. Board of Governors of the Federal Reserve System. "Total Loss-Absorbing Capacity, Long-Term Debt, and Clean Holding Company Requirements for Systemically Important U.S. Bank Holding Companies and Intermediate Holding Companies of Systemically Important Foreign Banking Organizations." *Federal Register (82 FR 8266)*. 24 January. Accessed August 30, 2018. https://www.federalregister.gov/documents/2017/01/24/2017-00431/total-loss-absorbing-capacity-long-term-debt-and-clean-holding-company-requirements-for-systemically.
FSB 2011a. Financial Stability Board. "Key Attributes of Effective Resolution Regimes for Financial Institutions." October. Financial Stability Board. https://www.financialstabilityboard.org/publications/r_111104cc.pdf.
FSB 2011b. Financial Stability Board. "Essential Elements of Institution-specific Cross-border Cooperation Agreements." 4 November. Accessed August 30, 2018. http://www.fsb.org/wp-content/uploads/I-Annex-2-Essential-Elements-of-Institution-specific-Cross-border-Cooperation-Agreements.pdf.
FSB 2014a. Financial Stability Board. "Key Attributes of Effective Resolution Regimes for Financial Institutions." 15 October. Accessed December 2015.
FSB 2014b. Financial Stability Board. "Adequacy of loss-absorbing capacity of global systemically important banks in resolution Consultative document." 10 November. Accessed June 2015. http://www.financialstabilityboard.org/wp-content/uploads/TLAC-Condoc-6-Nov-2014-FINAL.pdf.
FSB 2015a. Financial Stability Board. "Principles on Loss-absorbing and Recapitalisation Capacity of G-SIBs in Resolution: Total Loss-absorbing Capacity (TLAC) Term Sheet." 9 November. Accessed August 30, 2018. http://www.fsb.org/wp-content/uploads/TLAC-Principles-and-Term-Sheet-for-publication-final.pdf.
FSB 2015b. "Financial Stability Board. Principles for Cross-border Effectiveness of Resolution Actions." 3 November. Accessed August 30, 2018. http://www.fsb.org/wp-content/uploads/Principles-for-Cross-border-Effectiveness-of-Resolution-Actions.pdf.
FSB 2016a. Financial Stability Board. "Guidance on Arrangements to Support Operational Continuity in Resolution." 16 August. Accessed August 30, 2018. http://www.fsb.org/wp-content/uploads/Guidance-on-Arrangements-to-Support-Operational-Continuity-in-Resolution1.pdf.
FSB 2016b. Financial Stability Board. "Resilience through resolvability – moving from policy design to implementation: 5th Report to the G20 on progress in resolution." 18 August. Accessed August 30, 2018. http://www.fsb.org/wp-content/uploads/Resilience-through-resolvability-%E2%80%93-moving-from-policy-design-to-implementation.pdf.
FSB 2017a. Financial Stability Board. "Ten years on – taking stock of post-crisis resolution reforms: Sixth Report on the Implementation of Resolution Reforms." 6 July. Accessed August 30, 2018. http://www.fsb.org/wp-content/uploads/P060717-3.pdf.
FSB 2017b. Financial Stability Board. "Guidance on Continuity of Access to Financial Market Infrastructures ("FMIs") for a Firm in Resolution." 6 July. Accessed August 30, 2018. http://www.fsb.org/wp-content/uploads/P060717-2.pdf.
FSB 2017c. Financial Stability Board. "Funding Strategy Elements of an Implementable Resolution Plan." 30 November. Accessed August 30, 2018. http://www.fsb.org/wp-content/uploads/301117-2.pdf.

FSB 2018a. Financial Stability Board. "Monitoring the Technical Implementation of the FSB Total Loss-absorbing Capacity (TLAC) Standard: Call for public feedback." 6 June. Accessed August 30, 2018. http://www.fsb.org/wp-content/uploads/P060618.pdf.

FSB 2018b. Financial Stability Board. "Principles on Bail-in Execution." 21 June. Accessed August 30, 2018. http://www.fsb.org/wp-content/uploads/P210618-1.pdf.

G-20 2009. Group of 20. "Declaration on Strengthening the Financial System." April. Accessed December 2013. http://www.g20.utoronto.ca/2009/2009ifi.html.

Huertas, Thomas F. 2011. *Crisis: Cause, Containment and Cure*. 2nd. London: Palgrave Macmillan.

Huertas, Thomas F. 2016a. "How to deal with the resolution of financial market infrastructures."

Huertas, Thomas F. 2016b. "Six Structures in Search of Stability." Edited by Patricia Jackson. *Banking* Reform.https://www.suerf.org/studies/6507/banking-reform.

Huertas, Thomas F. 2018. "Calibrating capital: when will banks have enough?" *Banking Perspectives*. Accessed August 30, 2018. https://www.theclearinghouse.org/banking-perspectives/2018/2018-q2-banking-perspectives/articles/calibrating-capital.

Lee, Paul L. 2014. "Cross-Border Resolution of Banking Groups: International Initiatives and US Perspectives -- Part III." *Pratt's Journal of Bankruptcy Law* 291–335.

Lo, Andrew W. 2012. "Reading About the Financial Crisis: A Twenty-One-Book Review." 50 (1): 151–178. Accessed August 30, 2018. http:www.aeaweb.org/articles.php?doi=10.1257/jel.50.1.151.

Moody's Investor Services. 2014. "Moody's proposes revisions to its Bank Rating Methodology." 9 September. Accessed October 2014. https://www.moodys.com/research/Moodys-proposes-revisions-to-its-Bank-Rating-Methodology--PR_307938.

Tooze, Adam. 2018. *Crashed: How a Decade of Financial Crises Changed the World*. New York: Viking.

IV CCP Resolution

Steven Maijoor

Keynote: Resilience, recovery and resolution: Three essential Rs for CCPs

I am delighted to be in Frankfurt at this important conference and want to thank the Institute for Law and Finance for their kind invitation. This is a great opportunity to share with you some reflections on the important and complex topic of resolution. The timing of this discussion is especially relevant considering that the legislative process for the European framework for the resolution of CCPs is still ongoing.

We would all agree that European CCPs have become systemically important for the markets they clear and, through their interdependencies, for the European financial system as a whole – albeit some more than others. As for banks and insurance companies, a framework for the resolution of CCPs is needed in order to ensure the continuity of their critical services to preserve financial stability. Therefore, ESMA welcomes the Commission's proposal for a European framework for the recovery and resolution of CCPs.[1] As I have said before, CCPs without recovery and resolution plans are like vessels heading for the ocean, but without the lifeboats in place.

My first reflection is that the resolution framework for CCPs should not be considered in isolation, but in conjunction with the regulatory and supervisory framework applying to CCPs.

In the EU, the European Market Infrastructure Regulation[2] (EMIR) introduced regulatory requirements aimed at ensuring the *Resilience* of CCPs under extreme but plausible market conditions. Accordingly, among other things, CCPs have to:

- maintain pre-funded resources to cover default losses under extreme but plausible market conditions, including at least the default of the two biggest clearing members;

1 Proposal for a Regulation of the European Parliament and of the Council on a framework for the recovery and resolution of central counterparties (COM(2016) 856 final).

2 Regulation (EU) No 648/2012 of the European Parliament and of the Council of 4 July 2012 on OTC derivatives, central counterparties and trade repositories.

Steven Maijoor, Chair of ESMA

https://doi.org/10.1515/9783110644067-014

- meet capital requirements to protect itself against the risks of non- default losses, like operational, legal and business risks; and
- apply concentration limits to contain investment and custody losses.

The forthcoming European regulation for the recovery and resolution of CCPs will introduce specific regulatory requirements for *Recovery* of CCPs, which under the current proposal would remain subject to the supervision of the relevant national competent authority and to the review of CCP Colleges. Currently, in compliance with the Principles for Financial Market Infrastructures of the Committee on Payments and Market Infrastructures and the International Organization of Securities Commissions, CCPs are developing recovery plans to be able to address uncovered default losses beyond their pre-funded resources, as well as uncovered non-default losses.

Consequently, the *Resolution* of CCPs should focus on residual scenarios where a CCP is unable to implement its recovery plan or where the implementation of the recovery plan may negatively affect financial stability. A resolution plan should be designed around the specificities of a CCP's business, its balance sheet structure, and take into account the scenarios that could lead to the resolution of the CCP. The ultimate objective of any intervention of a resolution authority in such scenarios should be to ensure the continuity of critical services to preserve financial stability.

CCP Resilience, Recovery and Resolution are three essential "Rs" for CCPs, which are strictly interlinked: on the one hand, strong resilience arrangements can reduce the likelihood of the need for recovery and resolution. While, on the other hand, recovery and resolution arrangements should maintain incentives to ensure resilience in the Business-As-Usual (BAU) situation. In my speech today, I would like to share my thoughts on:

i. how to strengthen CCP resilience through ongoing supervision; and
ii. how to ensure that recovery and resolution arrangements support strong CCP resilience.

CCP resilience and supervision

In the EU, the resilience of CCPs is a key objective of the regulatory and supervisory framework established under EMIR. The supervision of EU CCPs is assigned to the designated national competent authority of the Member State where a CCP is established, while CCP colleges have been established to enable cooperation among all relevant authorities in the EU with a legitimate interest in the ongoing resilience of that CCP.

Furthermore, EMIR tasked ESMA with a key role in promoting supervisory convergence through its participation in all CCP colleges, the conduct of peer reviews, and the adoption of other supervisory convergence tools, such as Q&As, Opinions and Guidelines. Moreover, in order to assess the resilience of CCPs, ESMA conducts an EU-wide stress test considering macro-economic stress scenarios developed together with the ESRB.

EU-wide stress test

I can proudly say that ESMA is among the pioneers in developing methodologies and building expertise in this new frontier of Supervisory Stress Tests for CCPs. ESMA conducted the first ever credit stress test of CCPs in 2016, which focused on counterparty credit risk and interdependencies across CCPs. More recently, ESMA completed a second stress test exercise applying both credit *and* liquidity stress tests, including an improved methodological framework for the stress test scenario definition and the result validation. We also published for the first time the individual results of the credit stress tests.

The results of this recent exercise[3] confirmed that, overall, the system of EU CCPs is resilient to multiple clearing member defaults and extreme market shocks. However, for the credit tests the use of harmonised shocks permitted us to highlight differences in resilience between CCPs. This allowed us to identify minor failures of no systemic relevance for one CCP, and to highlight for another CCP a high sensitivity to marginal increases of the price shocks or the number of defaults, which may have systemic relevance. No systemic risk concerns were revealed by the liquidity stress tests.

ESMA's EU-wide stress tests represent a complementary supervisory tool allowing the assessment of the resilience of CCPs from a macro-perspective. The primary tools ensuring resilience are the supervision of the efficiency and soundness of a CCP risk management framework and, in particular, its individual stress test framework. In that context, the EMIR supervisory framework has been a solid part of the EU post-crisis regulatory response. However, even good products can be improved and upgraded, especially when facing a changing environment. Therefore, let me reflect on the ongoing review of EMIR and, in particular, the

3 See https://www.esma.europa.eu/press-news/esma-news/esma-publishes-results-second-eu-wide-ccp-stress-test.

proposal to strengthen the supervision of authorised EU-CCPs and recognised Third-Country CCPs (TC-CCPs), the so-called EMIR 2.2 proposal.[4]

CCP supervision under EMIR 2.2

Concerning *TC-CCPs*, ESMA welcomes the proposal to enhance the current recognition regime by introducing an enhanced regime for systemically important TC-CCPs, also referred to as Tier 2 CCPs.

The proposed new regime responds to the concerns raised by ESMA in 2015 in one of its reports on the EMIR review,[5] highlighting the limitations under the current recognition regime, whereby ESMA must fully rely on the supervision by the TC-CCP's home jurisdiction authority. While obviously not foreseen in 2015, the limitations of this "full deference" model would especially materialise after Brexit.

The proposed new EMIR 2.2 regime entrusts ESMA with direct supervisory tasks over recognised Tier 2 CCPs, which are then subject to the requirements for CCPs under EMIR. The new regime also envisages the possibility to apply for "comparable compliance" in cases where the compliance with the regulatory requirements in the home jurisdiction would satisfy the requirements for CCPs under EMIR. This dual regime is in line with the model applied in other jurisdictions outside the EU and it would clearly better serve the post-Brexit landscape.

Regarding *EU-CCPs*, the Commission proposal retains the current decentralised supervision by the relevant NCAs, but enhances ESMA's coordination role. For instance, it assigns ESMA the task to chair all CCP colleges and to provide its consent on specific supervisory decisions by a relevant National Competent Authority (NCA) on key CCP risk requirements.

As you are all aware, I can say, with some understatement, that especially when compared with the proposed role regarding TC-CCPs, not all member states are enthusiastic about giving ESMA a more important role in the supervision of EU-CCPs. While understanding some of the concerns, it is important to have the right balance between EU-CCP supervision and TC-CCP supervision. Only in that

4 Proposal for a regulation of the European Parliament and of the Council amending Regulation (EU) No 1095/2010 establishing a European Supervisory Authority (European Securities and Markets Authority) and amending Regulation (EU) No 648/2012 as regards the procedures and authorities involved for the authorisation of CCPs and requirements for the recognition of third-country CCPs (COM(2017) 331 final).

5 See EMIR Review Report no.4 of 13 August 2015 (ESMA/2015/1254).

way can we achieve the envisaged benefits in terms of scale and expertise, and this balance is also needed to ensure the credibility of EU supervision of TC-CPPs.

Let me take the opportunity to address one frequently heard argument against stronger EU CCP supervision, which is that as long as the resolution regime, which I will discuss later, will imply a fiscal impact on the member state where the CCP is located, the decision-making regarding CCPs should remain at national level.

However, I would like to note that the fiscal impact would never materialise if other recovery and resolution tools have effectively addressed any uncovered loss. Moreover, should the public financial support resolution tool be applied, this would cover only residual losses after other stakeholders, such as Clearing Members and CCP shareholders, beyond the national borders, had shared a substantial part of the initial losses. In this case, although the potential fiscal impact of a CCP resolution would remain in the Member State where the CCP is established, the economic impact of initial losses covered by prior recovery and resolution tools would have already affected other stakeholders across the EU.

Hence, considering the nature of CCPs, recovery and resolution inevitably imply loss sharing across borders. Hence, limiting the losses of a CCP to the member state where the CCP is located is an illusion. Therefore, it is crucial to ensure that CCP supervision does not only respond to the national interests of where the CCP is located, but preserves the interests of all relevant stakeholders. The CCP colleges have helped to enrich the perspectives considered by the relevant NCAs in supervising CCPs. Still, the proposed amendments in EMIR 2.2 would better preserve the interests of all stakeholders involved.

Now, let me highlight one important aspect of the EMIR 2.2 proposal that, in my view, should be considered further and it relates to the governance of ESMA. The original proposal introduced a new, and separate, governance structure for the tasks assigned to ESMA on CCPs under EMIR 2.2. This would effectively create another ESMA independent of the existing ESMA structure, which would continue to be responsible for single rule book activities and some supervisory convergence activities regarding CCPs.

I am not supportive of this new governance arrangement, for two reasons. First, as both governance bodies would be involved in CCP matters, there would be the risk of uncoordinated decisions, strategies, and communication. Second, especially when taking into account the review of the European Supervisory Authorities (ESA), it would make ESMA's governance top-heavy and inefficient with a total of nine executives.

Noting that the current governance of ESMA is also under discussion in the ESA review, we need to ensure that the ultimate arrangements are efficient, that all ESMA decisions and activities regarding CCPs are well coordinated, and that ESMA has an integrated strategy and communication. In that context, the proposal put forward to the Committee on Economic and Monetary Affairs of the European Parliament (ECON) by the Rapporteur of this dossier, MEP Danuta Huebner, is an important improvement.

I truly hope that EMIR 2.2 will progress on governance as it has done on improving the arrangements for the role of central banks. Considering the important links between CCPs, financial markets and monetary policy, it is imperative to ensure good cooperation between supervisors and central banks of issue. However, the original Commission proposals entailed the risk of deadlock as on a range of supervisory decisions the relevant national competent authority would have to seek the prior consent of both ESMA and the relevant central banks of issue.

Therefore, I very much welcome the recent amendment proposals being considered by the European Parliament, envisaging other cooperation arrangements, for instance, whereby ESMA would consult the relevant central banks of issue.

Finally, I would like to stress the importance of a timely adoption of EMIR 2.2. While the progress in the Brexit negotiations has resulted in an increased likelihood of a transitional regime, which is good news, it should not slow down the EMIR 2.2 legislative process. First, the transition regime is not yet certain, and there is still the risk that the UK-CCPs' authorisations as EU-CCPs expire by the end of March 2019. Second, even when the transition regime ultimately comes into place, it will only delay the expiration date to the end of December 2020. By that time, the EU should have a functioning supervisory system for systematically important third- country CCPs, which is difficult to envisage if EMIR 2.2 is only agreed after the next parliamentary elections.

CCP recovery and resolution

Turning to the core topic of today's conference, I want to recall the main differences between recovery and resolution, which in my opinion should be reflected in the resolution framework for CCPs. A key difference between the two relates to the responsible actor. Whereas recovery is the responsibility of a CCP, resolution is under the responsibility of resolution authorities. However, there are further important differences.

Different perspectives and objectives

Recovery has a micro-perspective and the objective is to maintain the CCP's viability as a going concern and to ensure the continuity of critical services.

Recovery needs to address any uncovered loss, liquidity shortfall or capital inadequacy, arising from a participant default or other non- default causes, such as business, operational or other structural weaknesses.

On the other hand, the macro-perspective objective of resolution is to pursue financial stability, ensuring the continuity of critical services, either by restoring the ability of the CCP to perform those functions as a going concern or ensuring the performance of those functions by another entity or arrangement, coupled with the orderly wind-down of the CCP in resolution.

These different perspectives of recovery and resolution can result in a different classification of critical services and different strategies. Recovery should address all critical services essential to the viability of the CCP, while resolution should focus only on those critical services essential to preserve financial stability. This can lead to different strategies with respect to what services and business lines should be continued or wound-down.

Different scenarios

As I mentioned earlier, recovery should address scenarios where uncovered loss, liquidity shortfall or capital inadequacy, arise in unpredictable market circumstances beyond extreme, but plausible market conditions.

Resolution should then consider those most severe default and non- default scenarios where a CCP is not able to implement its recovery plan or where the implementation of the recovery plan may negatively affect financial stability. Resolution plans should be developed taking into account the constraints emerging under such scenarios.

Different tools

Resolution authorities should have the power to exercise all recovery tools envisaged in the CCP recovery plan, as reflected in the applicable CCP rules and other contractual arrangements. This is particularly relevant in those scenarios where the CCP is not able to implement its recovery plan.

Depending on the actual circumstances, the resolution authority should be enabled to implement the recovery plan, to the extent that this serves financial stability.

Moreover, resolution authorities should be empowered with additional resolution tools to address those scenarios where recovery tools are not sufficient to ensure the continuity of the CCP's critical services for financial stability.

Against this background, I want to raise two "unresolved" questions on the resolution of CCPs and, without intending to pre-empt the discussion at the next Panel debate, I will provide my answers.

When should a resolution authority intervene?

The proposal for a European Regulation on CCP Recovery and Resolution envisages that a resolution authority should intervene when the following three cumulative conditions apply. First, the relevant competent authority or resolution authority, after consulting each other, shall determine that the CCP is "failing or likely to fail"; second, there is no reasonable prospect that alternative private sector measures or supervisory actions would prevent the failure of the CCP; and third, a resolution action is necessary in the public interest to preserve financial stability.

With respect to the first condition, the proposal for the Regulation envisages a mandate to ESMA to issue guidelines to determine the detailed circumstances under which a CCP shall be considered as failing or likely to fail. These guidelines would promote the convergence of supervisory and resolution authorities' determination of when the resolution of a CCP should be triggered.

Given the advancing legislative process, ESMA has initiated preparatory work for drafting these guidelines. We need to consider when a CCP shall be deemed to be failing or likely to fail. This would, for instance, include circumstances where the CCP infringes its authorisation requirements, becomes unable to provide a critical function or to pay its liabilities as they fall due, or to restore its viability through the implementation of its recovery measures. Please be assured that ESMA will seek the views of all relevant stakeholders through a public consultation in due course.

Who should cover the losses in resolution?

Understandably, this has always been a hotly debated issue. I believe that, as a general principle, the resolution authorities should seek to adhere to the CCP's recovery plan to the largest possible extent in order not to alter the distribution of uncovered losses between its clearing members and shareholders, as contractually agreed.

However, in cases where the recovery tools would not serve the resolution objectives under the actual circumstances triggering the resolution of a CCP, the resolution authority should cautiously determine what alternative resolution tools to apply, in line with its resolution plan. In particular, the resolution authority should take into account the impact these tools would have on the stakeholders involved.

While fully recognising the need to introduce important safeguards, such as the "no creditor worse off" principle, it is equally important that the resolution planning does not alter the incentives to the relevant stakeholders to contribute to an effective default management under, first, business-as-usual and, then, recovery.

Therefore, I welcome the resolution principles introduced in the proposal for Regulation on CCP Recovery and Resolution, and in particular the condition that any resolution tool based on public financial support to a CCP in resolution should be used as a last resort. Indeed, the proposal provides for a very rich set of resolution tools that should generally allow resolution authorities to handle both default and non-default scenarios without the need to rely on taxpayers' money.

I would like to conclude my speech here and look forward to discussing further these and other "unresolved" questions with the other distinguished members on the next panel. I am confident that this debate provides a valuable contribution to the European co-legislators in identifying appropriate and balanced answers for the finalisation of the forthcoming European Regulation on CCP Recovery and Resolution.

Benoît Cœuré

A cooperative approach to CCP recovery and resolution

The order of the topics at today's conference on "resolution in Europe" was well planned.[1] The fact that we are discussing central counterparty (CCP) resolution after discussing bank resolution echoes the fact that CCP resolution is, by and large, an event that occurs only when all other safeguards, including bank resolution, have failed.

There are a number of reasons for this.

One is that the ways in which CCPs are set up makes them particularly resilient. CCPs are not banks, they are (financial market) infrastructures.

They manage the risk of a matched book and rely on the strength of their membership to provide margin and to share losses if this proves insufficient. Bail-in is integral to CCPs' operational set-up, as clearing members are required to share losses. In this way, their resilience is further strengthened by banking supervision and recovery and resolution arrangements which help ensure that clearing members meet their obligations.

Another reason for CCPs' resilience is the implementation of international standards.[2] The Principles for Financial Markets Infrastructures of the Committee on Payments and Market Infrastructures (CPMI) and the International Organization of Securities Commissions (IOSCO) have recently benefitted from more granular guidance providing clarity to CCPs and their regulators.[3]

---

1 I would like to thank Corinna Freund for her contributions to this article. I remain solely responsible for the opinions contained herein.

2 At all times, CCPs are required to hold prefunded, high quality collateral to cover 99% of current and potential losses that may arise from their participants defaulting. On top of this, they need to hold additional resources to withstand a range of extreme but plausible stress scenarios. These could include, for instance, the two largest participants in a major cross-border CCP defaulting. To prepare for situations of even more extreme market distress, CCPs also need to formulate recovery plans that show how they intend to absorb losses and restore business viability. See Cœuré, B. (2015), "Ensuring an adequate loss-absorbing capacity of central counterparties," remarks at the Federal Reserve Bank of Chicago 2015 Symposium on Central Clearing, Chicago, 10 April.

3 See CPMI-IOSCO (2017), "Recovery of financial market infrastructures – Revised report", July.

Benoît Cœuré, Member of the Executive Board of the ECB, at the ILF Conference on "Resolution in Europe: the unresolved questions", Frankfurt am Main, 23 April 2018

https://doi.org/10.1515/9783110644067-015

This also includes risks other than financial ones. The adoption of the CPMI-IOSCO guidance on cyber resilience for financial market infrastructures, for example, is an important step towards operational resilience.[4]

Yet, while CCP resolution remains a very unlikely event, the disorderly failure of a major CCP would be disastrous.

Many CCPs are globally systemic, responsible for clearing global markets and with participants from across the world. This is why the Financial Stability Board (FSB) guidance on central counterparty resolution, and its focus on planning and cooperation between authorities, is important.

Cooperation in resolution planning, and co-ordination between recovery and resolution planning, is essential to ensure that a CCP is always able to continue performing its systemically relevant functions across all concerned jurisdictions.

I also welcome the fact that policy discussion is now scrutinising seriously the wisdom of increased top-down prefunding requirements for CCP resolution. It is doubtful that such requirements would be effective or proportionate, given the very low probability of CCP resolution and the marked differences between CCPs' risk profiles.

What is more, increasing funding requirements could discourage the use of CCPs and instead push counterparties towards riskier and more opaque bilateral clearing. And while I would not exclude cases where additional financial resources should be available for both recovery and resolution, ring-fencing resources *for resolution only* may distort the incentives of all stakeholders to support a successful recovery.

That said, the resolution authority should have flexibility to determine the optimal choice of available tools, as well as the best point in time for entry into resolution, as long as the "no creditor worse off" principle is respected.

It is helpful to assess how further guidance could support authorities in assessing potential resolution funding needs for individual CCPs, taking into account, for example, the specific risk characteristics of the products they clear, the types of market they serve and the concentration in CCP memberships. I fully support work currently under way in the FSB in this respect.

In this article, I would like to focus on three key areas where more work is needed.

---

4 See CPMI-IOSCO (2016), "Guidance on cyber resilience for financial market infrastructures", June. The Eurosystem recently established the Euro Cyber Resilience Board (ECRB) for pan-European Financial Infrastructures, which will help raise awareness and provide a platform for discussing issues related to cybersecurity. See Cœuré, B. (2018), "A Euro Cyber Resilience Board for pan-European Financial Infrastructures", introductory remarks at the first meeting of the ECRB, Frankfurt, 9 March.

First, more international cooperation is needed

Authorities responsible for several major cross-border CCPs have not yet embarked on resolution planning and no cross-border crisis management arrangements are yet in place.[5]

This could be because of barriers to sharing confidential information, including different approaches as to what is considered confidential and what timely. If that is true, then these barriers need to be removed.

Likewise, authorities may be reticent to engage with others while legislative frameworks are still evolving. Assessing the cross-border implications of a CCP resolution takes time and discussions should get under way as soon as possible.

CPMI and IOSCO are conducting some work in this respect.

Second, authorities need to better understand how a CCP resolution might look like

CCP resolution scenarios cannot be defined in absolute, quantitative terms given the nature of market events causing resolution. There will always be considerable uncertainty around CCP resolution and related funding needs.

Nevertheless, further steps should be taken to improve the analytical foundation of CCP resolution planning and to better prepare authorities.

While the FSB is addressing this issue in its report, I see two steps in particular.

First, CPMI and IOSCO have recently published guidance for supervisory stress testing, which includes guidance on how multiple authorities can conduct stress tests.[6] Testing a CCP's recovery plan by authorities may help to assess the market conditions under which recovery – and potentially resolution – may be necessary, as well as the potential funding required. Internationally coordinated stress-testing is essential to foster a better understanding of the aggregate amount and quality of committed funding that is available across major CCPs.

---

5 Under the FSB Key Attributes of Effective Resolution Regimes, FSB members have committed to establish crisis management groups for CCPs that are systemically important in more than one jurisdiction.

6 See CPMI-IOSCO (2018), "Framework for supervisory stress testing of central counterparties (CCPs)", April.

Co-ordinating CCP and banking stress testing will provide additional understanding on how resolution plans would work in case of extreme scenarios.

Second, recent analysis of central clearing interdependencies carried out by the standard-setting committees has revealed the limited number of banking groups that are members of CCPs across the world, thereby closely linking CCPs themselves.[7]

Even without stress testing, it is easy to understand that a CCP under stress would send a liquidity shockwave across its participants and beyond as it requires additional margins and/or passes on losses. This is especially important for central banks. With stress testing, potential funding strains can be further explored, and useful information for CCP and bank supervisors as well as resolution authorities can be gleaned.

Third, European arrangements for CCP recovery and resolution must be coordinated

The significant interdependencies between CCPs globally are also present in the Single Market. Resolution planning should therefore be coordinated across all European Union CCPs.[8] This is crucial to preserve financial stability within the Union in the event of a crisis.

Critics of EU-wide coordination claim that the fiscal risks of central clearing arise primarily in CCPs' respective home countries. But given that cross-border membership of EU banks in EU CCPs is widespread, this argument is flawed.

The losses faced by a CCP during default management and recovery and resolution are mostly borne by its clearing members, rather than by the CCP itself. Even though a CCP's home country may choose to provide temporary public funding during resolution, such support would be recouped from clear-

7 See BCBS, CPMI, FSB and IOSCO (2017), "Analysis of central clearing interdependencies", 5 July.

8 See also ECB (2017), Opinion of the European Central Bank on a proposal for a regulation of the European Parliament and of the Council on a framework for the recovery and resolution of central counterparties and amending Regulations (EU) No 1095/2010, (EU) No 648/2012, and (EU) 2015/2365 (CON/2017/38), 20 September.

ing members, in line with their obligations to contribute to comprehensive loss absorption.

Therefore, fiscal risks would in fact appear to arise in countries in which major CCP *participants* are located. Domestic authorities may need to provide these participants with financial support if they are faced with large payment obligations due to CCP losses.

Thus, EU-wide coordination in resolution planning is necessary to ensure that system-wide risks are fully identified and mitigated in a fair and effective manner.

At the same time, a resolution is not a discrete event. The boundaries between default management and recovery and resolution are blurred, so it is important to align responsibilities and control measures throughout the potential lifecycle of EU CCPs.

The resolution of a CCP relies, to a large extent, on the recovery process. Under the legislative proposal for a regulation on CCP recovery and resolution, authorities will be required to enforce CCPs' contractual obligations before using any resolution tools, subject to limited exemptions.

Another aspect to keep in mind is that systemic risk for the Single Market may arise not only from EU CCPs, but also from non-EU CCPs with substantial activities in the EU. This aspect will become increasingly important after the United Kingdom's departure from the EU.

Against this background, current efforts to strengthen the EU arrangements for third country CCPs are very important. In particular, if a third country CCP is systemically important for the EU, it is not enough to focus on regulatory equivalence alone.

While deference to home country rules and supervisors should be used to the extent possible, EU authorities also need to have tools for direct liaison with a third country CCP to identify, clarify and address issues that may pose specific concerns from an EU financial stability perspective. This is fully in line with the set up in other major jurisdictions.

Similarly, as regards CCP resolution, the development of home country arrangements in line with international standards must be complemented with the involvement of relevant EU authorities in resolution planning in line with international standards, to ensure that their systemic risk concerns are fully taken into account.

To sum up, CCPs are systemically important across border and across the EU. Any recovery and resolution planning for individual CCPs therefore requires an EU wide systemic risk assessment and a strong co-ordination at global level.

At EU level, this could involve, for instance, aggregated data collection, joint stress-testing and crisis simulation exercises, and the closer coordination of related supervisory assessments and recovery and resolution planning. And given the financial stability, macroprudential and liquidity issues a CCP resolution raises, central banks must be involved in all aspects of this work.

Joachim Faber

Building on the achievements of the G20 reforms

With the outbreak of the financial crisis in 2007, supervisory arrangements proved insufficient and deficiencies in the risk management of the financial industry became apparent. More than a decade later, there is merit in reminding ourselves how much society suffered from the consequences.

It was against this background that the G20 committed to bringing OTC markets towards more stability, mainly by introducing the obligation to collateralize most risk exposures and centrally clear certain products.

The primary aim of post-crisis regulation in the EU and worldwide is to protect taxpayers' money. We as Deutsche Börse Group appreciate the great efforts from the regulators having seen various regulatory initiatives that have contributed to achieving this objective.

Let me highlight the following two points: First, bank regulation. There can be no doubt that capital requirements and collateral requirements (CRD IV / CRR) as well as the requirement to maintain recovery and resolution plans (BRRD) have contributed to the resilience of banks.

And, secondly, for CCPs in particular, this meant they were entrusted to become the independent risk managers of financial markets – a critically important decision for our society.

The EU introduced highest standards for CCPs with the implementation of the European Market Infrastructure Regulation (EMIR). EMIR has significantly improved the systemic stability of financial markets – as for example witnessed on 24 June 2016 following the Brexit referendum. While market swings were similar to the ones in relation to the default of Lehman Brothers, markets remained sound and stable.

We at Deutsche Börse are convinced that the EMIR is an excellent regulation which has greatly contributed to achieving a healthy and effective incentive structure thanks to the thorough implementation of the G20 agenda in whole by the EU regulators. At the same time, we all should be aware of the widely considered systemic importance CCPs have reached mainly due to the clearing obligation. It is therefore the right and logical next step to develop a recovery and resolution legislation also for CCPs as the missing piece of the regulatory framework. Regulatory efforts going into the development of CCP recovery and

Joachim Faber, Chairman of the Supervisory Board, Deutsche Börse AG

https://doi.org/10.1515/9783110644067-016

resolution regulation will add the missing piece to the regulatory framework. CCP recovery and resolution is covering extreme but plausible scenarios in stress testing under the circumstance that banking rules fail and installed EMIR safeguards prove insufficient.

The EU Commission's legislative proposal is an excellent groundwork and the European Parliament's position contains many changes that will be highly beneficial to financial market stability. Nonetheless, we as a market infrastructure provider want to stress some points that appear particularly important to achieving the objective of improving financial markets stability.

The regulation should, firstly, clearly highlight the last resort character of public funds and stipulate their temporary and refundable nature in order avoid moral hazard and protect the taxpayer. Secondly, increasing the weight of CCP equity in the line of defence brings incentives out of balance. The CCP has a natural interest in a successful recovery as it is at risk to lose everything if recovery fails. At the same time increasing CCP's contribution to recovery would weaken market participants' incentive to contribute to a successful recovery. A third point: Compensating clearing members for the participation in loss allocation on recovery is a dramatic and unjustified removal of the participant-based loss sharing and breaks the incentive structure. It appears unfair to exempt the risk takers in the CCP system who benefit significantly from CCP services under normal market conditions.

This way, a coherent and well-functioning interplay between most relevant CCP regulations will maintain the existing and healthy incentive structure. And as such it will contribute to improving financial markets stability.

However, CCPs should have a stake (i.e. "skin in the game") in the lines of defence in order to ensure they are properly incentivised to run an efficient risk management system. But we strongly believe that the current set up under EMIR creates a balanced incentive structure whereby both the Clearing Members and the CCP are incentivised to participate in the rebalancing of the CCP unmatched book as both may have losses to face. Vice versa: it is not the duty of any CCP to encourage (e.g. by another balance of collateral) the taking of risks by its members.

To give an example: Eurex Clearing own in the lines of defence amount to € 150 mn, which is roughly one third of Eurex Clearing Equity Capital. This constitutes a strong incentive for Eurex Clearing to run an efficient risk management, which is the intention behind such "skin in the game".

This is not the place to go into greater detail. In any case, the impact of transforming the balance between the CCP and its members is likely to be strong. Currently, the CCP has the biggest natural interest in a successful recovery, as the expectation is that it will lose everything if recovery fails. But on the other hand increasing CCP contribution to recovery (in particular when contributions are made at the very beginning of the recovery phase before clearing has anything to contribute) would weaken market participants' incentive to take part in a successful recovery. In other words: more equity capital in the system not necessarily strengthen its robustness.

For financial stability purposes, the first and foremost objective of this regulation should be to ensure that the losses remaining after voluntary auction process are as small as possible, before addressing their allocation. EMIR is making excellent progress, if this fine balance is maintained.

To sum up, the current setup under EMIR should be continued as it creates a balanced incentive structure whereby both the clearing members and the CCP are equally encouraged to participate in the rebalancing of the CCP unmatched book as both may have losses to face.

Daniel Maguire

Considerations on CCP resolution planning

Despite the very different nature and functions of CCPs and banking institutions, parallels between their resolution regimes are often drawn. However, if these institutions are part of the same ecosystem, their fairly different nature and roles should be taken into consideration when determining the most appropriate remedies to their respective entry into resolution.

The link that can be drawn between the resolution of CCPs and banking institutions is not one of similarities but a link due to a causal effect: the entry into resolution of a CCP could theoretically be triggered by the resolution of several of its member banks. Indeed, the entry into resolution of a CCP would not happen in isolation. It would follow several defaults of banking institutions facing the CCP, that banking authorities would not have been in a position to avoid.[1] CCPs are important nodes in the market, but more importantly they are part of a broader ecosystem. Any event affecting them would also reflect the broader state of the marketplace. Their role benefits the wider system and directly reflects the need to break contagion and mutualise risk – especially when CCPs are internationally mutualised and subject to multiple supervision.

When considering CCP resolution mechanisms, it is vital to keep in mind these aspects, central to the understanding of CCP resolution mechanism.

CCPs need specific resolution regimes

In a number of jurisdictions, the definition of CCP resolution regimes is being discussed following the definition of resolution regimes for banking institutions, particularly those that are considered "*too big to fail*". For example, the directive on bank recovery and resolution was adopted in May 2014[2] while the

1 We will focus in this article on the issues linked to the default of one of several CCP clearing members, the so-called 'default losses'.

2 Directive 2014/59/EU of the European Parliament and of the Council of 15 May 2014 establishing a framework for the recovery and resolution of credit institutions and investment firms of the European Parliament and of the Council.

Daniel Maguire, Chief Executive Officer, LCH Group

https://doi.org/10.1515/9783110644067-017

Proposal of the European Commission on a CCP recovery and resolution regime[3] is still being discussed by the co-legislators.[4]

This has led to parallels being drawn between the two regimes and the concept that resolution regimes for banks could be transposed to the functions operated by CCPs.

However, CCPs and banking institutions fulfil completely different functions and their resolution needs to be approached in a completely different manner. Contrary to banking institutions, the core role and function of a CCP is to manage the risk created in the market, specifically the risk generated by risk-taking activities of its members:

- Clearing members (mostly banking institutions) enter into transactions and are responsible for introducing the corresponding risk to the market. This is reflected by the fact that clearing members – as risk-takers – provide the vast majority of the resources in the CCP's default waterfall: margins and default fund contributions. These resources are calibrated on the risk stemming from their transactions, in order to ensure the CCP has sufficient loss absorption capacity in case of clearing member default.
- CCPs ensure that their members manage their own risks appropriately: the CCP's primary responsibility is to organise risk mitigation procedures and adequately set margin levels and default fund requirements. CCPs are risk mutualisation vehicles critical to break contagion and ensure the continuity of systems. CCPs have the primary responsibility of organising a risk mitigation procedure and adequately setting margin levels and default fund requirements.

These elements are important when defining the resolution regime of CCPs: these regimes need to be adapted to the very nature of the entity assessed.

The core function of a CCP is precisely not to be exposed to market risk (to run a "*flat book*"). They are not risk takers, they are risk managers. Likewise, CCP resolution regimes are not about addressing the new "*too big to fail*" institutions: the "*too big to fail*" institutions remain the same (the members) and CCPs ensure that the risks stemming from their activities are managed by mutualisation mechanisms that proved their resilience during the financial crisis. CCPs as institutions are critical because they manage the risks represented by risk-taking activities.

---

3 Proposal for a Regulation of the European Parliament and of the Council on a framework for the recovery and resolution of central counterparties and amending Regulations (EU) No 1095/2010, (EU) No 648/2012, and (EU) 2015/2365.

4 The Proposal was published by the European Commission on 28.11.2016.

This is why CCPs are rightfully referred to as the ultimate "*circuit breakers*" which help safely mutualise and spread the effects of a default: CCPs break vertical risk coming from a handful of entities into multiple horizontal losses sharing through mutualisation and by doing so, stop contagion and dilute the shock on the overall system and ultimately the real economy.

CCPs need fully independent risk management

Regulators encourage clearing through CCPs specifically because of this mutualisation role, because of the greater transparency and safety central clearing brings compared to bilateral transactions.

In particular, CCPs are a backstop in case of default, an additional layer that ensures that any default is managed without recourse to taxpayers' money. This is ensured by a robust and prudent risk management as well as a default waterfall based on a strong incentive structure. In particular the default waterfall structure of a CCP ensures that:

- Defaulters pay first: the defaulter's margins are first in line to cover its losses and assist the liquidation of its portfolio. For example, at LCH the Initial margins are calibrated to be sufficient to offset any losses under normal market conditions incurred during the close-out period of a clearing member default, to a 99.7% confidence level (which is beyond EMIR requirements[5]).
- The CCP is further incentivised to calibrate adequately the resources of each clearing member as it would be the first hit in the case the losses were the resources of a defaulter not be sufficient to cover its losses (so called "*skin in the game*").
- The members contribute to the vast majority of the resources in the CCP's default waterfall (margins and default fund contributions) as they are the ones bringing risks to the system.
- Additional mechanisms are put in place to incentivise clearing members to contribute to the liquidation of the defaulter's portfolio: for e.g. the use of non-defaulter's default fund contribution can be based on the behaviour in auctions.

5 COMMISSION DELEGATED REGULATION (EU) No 153/2013 of 19 December 2012 supplementing Regulation (EU) No 648/2012 of the European Parliament and of the Council with regard to regulatory technical standards on requirements for central counterparties – Article 24.

By its size and incentives structure, CCPs default waterfall provides a prescriptive process for managing extreme tail events. Its execution is central in ensuring these incentives are maintained. It is therefore crucial to preserve the CCPs' default waterfall and its independent execution as it is integral to the CCPs' ability to fully allocate losses and return to a matched book in case of a clearing member's default. This preservation is critical to the CCP's credibility under Business As Usual and maintains an adequate incentive structure. The resolution process should not as a principle, interfere with its execution.

In addition it is central, when assessing the resolvability of a CCP, to ensure that it has a risk management that is fully independent. For example, CCPs cannot rely solely on central bank liquidity to manage their risks. An independent access to adequate liquidity resources is essential for a CCP and such liquidity can be derived from several sources. For example: EMIR is clear on the fact that "*in assessing the adequacy of liquidity resources, especially in stress situations, a CCP should take into consideration the risks of obtaining the liquidity by only relying on commercial banks credit lines*". It is always up to central banks to grant such liquidity on the said day: there is no and must be no "*right*" to Central Bank liquidity. This independent risk management is central to CCP resilience and their central role in addressing broader market turmoil.

CCP resolution regimes cannot be defined in isolation

As discussed above, CCPs and banks are very different in nature and functions. They are part of the same "*ecosystem*" but have a very different role in it. Being part of the same ecosystem, there is necessarily a link between the resolution of the banking sector and how it can affect a CCP. It is therefore important to understand the causes of a potential entry into resolution of a CCP, and the link with the resolution of the banking sector especially when it comes to so-called "*default losses*" (losses incurred by the default of one or several clearing members).

The resolution of a CCP would not happen as an isolated event – it would be the last step of significantly widespread market turmoil, including the resolution of several other actors, all of which would have had to be in resolution and fail to recover. These actors would include banking institutions of course, but also potentially a wider range of entities, such as sovereigns.

To get a sense of scale of the extreme scenario CCP resolution regimes would seek to address, there is no better example than the very one that triggered the reforms made by regulators around the globe as a result of the financial crisis: Lehman Brothers' default.

Lehman Brothers' default caused huge market turmoil and significantly tested markets' financial stability. For LCH, Lehman defaults meant the management of approximatively a $9 trillion portfolio of Interest rates swaps, 66,390 trades, as well as futures, cash and repos. Still, the consequences of this default were managed using a portion of Lehman's initial margins across all of their assets held at LCH (which is the first layer of the risk waterfall), and more importantly without using any of the mutualisation mechanisms pre-existing within the CCP or any of the CCP contribution. The default was fully resolved, well within the pre-funded margins of the defaulter held at the CCP and at no loss to other market participants, meaning that the pre-funded default fund remained untouched, very far from any recovery or resolution tools.

In addition, since Lehman Brothers' default happened, regulators around the globe introduced several measures that reinforce the resilience of the mutualised "*ecosystem*", making both banks and CCPs more resilient. Concerning the European Union, these improvements were mainly introduced via:

- The reinforcement of banks' capital, recovery and resolution through CRD[6]/CRR[7] (including the leverage capital ratio) and BRRD[8] which added an additional layer to deal with the banks' default.
- The reinforcement of CCPs' risk management requirements through EMIR,[9]
- Individual additional resilience standards as some CCPs have chosen to set their risk management requirements even beyond EMIR standards. This is the case of LCH Group's CCPs.

The ecosystem is far more capitalised and insulated than it was in 2008. CCP resolution regimes therefore aim to prepare for the tail of the tail risk, a series of failures that would be so unprecedented that all these mechanisms would

---

6 Directive 2013/36/EU of the European Parliament and of the Council of 26 June 2013 on access to the activity of credit institutions and the prudential supervision of credit institutions and investment firms, amending Directive 2002/87/EC and repealing Directives 2006/48/EC and 2006/49/EC.

7 Regulation (EU) No 575/2013 of the European Parliament and of the Council of 26 June 2013 on prudential requirements for credit institutions and investment firms and amending Regulation 648/2012.

8 Directive 2014/59/EU of the European Parliament and of the Council of 15 May 2014 establishing a framework for the recovery and resolution of credit institutions and investment firms of the European Parliament and of the Council.

9 Regulation (EU) No 648/2012 of the European Parliament and of the Council of 4 July 2012 on OTC derivatives, central counterparties and trade repositories.

prove insufficient to preserve several banks from defaulting and the CCP from exhausting all of its default waterfall resources. Indeed, before effecting the CCP "*skin in the game*" or non-defaulter's resources (default fund), a series of events going further than the "*extreme but plausible market conditions*" defined under EMIR[10] would have to happen:

1. One (or several) banking institution have defaulted despite the application of CRD/CRR stringent requirements improving banking sector resilience.
2. The overall banking resolution framework has proven insufficient, or it has been decided by the relevant authorities to let the said banking institution go into default, judging that it would either not be in a position to resolve the said banking institution or that, at this specific stage, allowing the banking institution to fail on the CCP was the most appropriate approach for the clearing ecosystem.
3. The risk models of the CCP approved by regulators have completely failed and proven insufficient to cover this particular member's default: as a reminder CCPs will have stringent risk models ensuring that they can manage the default of a member within its own initial margins and these risk models are scrutinised by regulators (the national competent authority, ESMA and the College of supervisors). For example the total initial margin held by UK CCPs against derivatives has more than doubled over the last five years with average levels at £145 billion at end 2017.[11]
4. The application of the cover 2 standard[12] has proved insufficient, meaning that more than the two largest clearing members of the CCP have failed simultaneously and their own initial margins were insufficient in covering their losses.
5. CCPs, CCPs' supervisors – including central banks (Bank of England and the Autorité de contrôle prudentiel et de résolution – Banque de France for LCH Group) – and even ESMA EU-wide stress-tests[13] and going beyond extreme but plausible scenarios have not prepared the CCPs for such shock.
6. CCPs' additional tools such as cash calls (assessment), variation margin haircutting etc. have also proven insufficient.

---

10 Article 42 of EMIR.

11 Bank of England FMI annual report 2017.

12 EMIR Article 42 (3) imposes the default fund EU CCPs to withstand the default of the clearing member to which it has the biggest exposure or of the second and third largest members if their exposure is larger.

13 Conducted pursuant to Article 21 (6) (b) of EMIR.

This would therefore require way more than any "*extreme but plausible market conditions*" to come close to a CCP recovery, let alone its resolution – way beyond what we have been able to model over the last decade.

This series of failure would, by definition, be of extreme magnitude and affect many entities, involve several authorities before actually affecting the CCP default management. This would imply the spreading of defaults so largely across clearing members (banking institutions) that the prevention and resolution measures from their own regulatory regime and authorities' supervision did not prove effective and that cooperation between banking authorities did not work either, to reach the stage where the CCP's dedicated resources can be affected; a situation where the resolution authorities of banking institutions have not been in a position to avoid contagion effects to the CCP.

Such a material series of events is very unlikely to be an isolated, local issue that is managed by one authority in isolation. Successful resolution will necessarily involve multiple jurisdictions and their authorities.

So at this stage the question is how should we manage the resolution of a CCP when the underlying causes are necessarily market-wide, cross border, a complete meltdown of financial markets that has not been foreseen even in worse cases scenarios including in EU wide stress tests?

For this reason, discussions and debates around the resilience, recovery and resolution of a CCP cannot be treated in isolation: there is a need to put some perspective around the resolution of CCPs in order to properly select the tools and the mechanisms which will truly be effective for regulators and for market participants in such specific exceptional circumstances for e.g. by involving different regulators and supervisors representing the diversity of CCP membership pre-crisis to ensure the effectiveness of any CCP resolution.

CCPs are nodes in the market, and part of a broader ecosystem. Any event affecting them would also reflect the broader state of the marketplace. CCPs are not isolated, on the contrary they break contagion thus sit in the middle and are reflecting the overall environment.

Since a CCP handling a major default would be the direct symptom of much bigger problems in the financial system, it would require strong cooperation and involvement of authorities on a cross-border basis, not only to ensure the management of the resolution of a CCP, but to manage the multiple resolutions at stake which led to this situation – including the resolution of defaulting clearing members.

The involvement and cooperation of different regulators and supervisors in the supervision of CCPs representing the diversity of CCP membership pre-crisis will be critical to ensure the effectiveness of resolution.

These cooperation mechanisms should ensure the enforceability of CCP resilience, recovery and resolution tools which would ensure a smoother management of a crisis. This would also avoid *ex-ante* strong divergences in the application of CCP resilience, recovery and resolution tools across jurisdictions. These cooperation mechanisms should cover a wide range of issues in order to bring as much clarity as possible upfront:

(a) the coordination of supervisory activities, including the exchange of information and reporting concerning changes to risk models and parameters, extension of CCP activities and services that substantially affect the CCP and its clearing members;
(b) the coordination of supervisory activities in case of a default of a clearing member's clients or indirect clients;
(c) the consultation of the relevant authorities of clearing members' resolution authorities in drawing up the resolution plan of the CCP;
(d) the coordination of recovery and resolution activities in cases where the CCP uses or intends to use recovery tools.;
(e) the notification of ESMA and relevant Member States' resolution authorities when a CCP is deemed to be failing or likely to fail.

In the kind of unprecedented events that would trigger a CCP to come close to a resolution, the CCP role would precisely be to fulfil its core function and mutualise the effects of a default coming from a handful of entities into multiple horizontal loss sharing through mutualisation supported by regulators.

There is an advantage for regulators and markets as they allow mutualisation of risk and of regulators' supervision, central to any successful resolution. This mutualisation of risks is central to any successful resolution and can only be effective if the "*clearing ecosystem*" including CCP members and their supervisors are committed to a non-discriminatory system to deal with this mutualisation of risks.

This is why cooperation is key when we talk about CCP resolution: CCP resolution will necessarily need to be put in a broader context. This broader context will need to be managed by a number of authorities, representing the multiple entities at stake in this financial crisis.

International mutualised diverse CCPs with multiple supervision and wide ranging coordinated resolution planning represent a benefit to the wider system and directly reflect the need to break contagion and mutualise risk. We believe these benefits are reinforced by strong ex-ante cooperation arrangements between regulators to ensure the coordination and enforceability of resolution regimes as ultimately it is critical that a CCP is able to perform its functions.

Levin Holle

Resolution of CCPs

1 Introduction

Clearing houses are one of the most important entities within the system of financial market infrastructures. The significance of CCPs has been emphasized since September 2009, when G20 leaders agreed that all standardized over the counter (OTC) derivatives contracts should be cleared through a central counterparty (CCP) by the end of 2012, with the aim of making these transactions more resistant to shocks and achieving greater transparency. This agreement was an aftermath of the financial crisis. These goals were transposed in the EU by EMIR, which was published in the Official Journal of the European Union in July 2012 (Regulation 648/2012, OJ L 201, 27. 7. 2012, p. 1).

The application of these new rules brought up new concerns because of the risk concentration in the CCPs. For the clearing members, a CCP is the buyer to every seller as well as also being the seller to every buyer. A CCP has a central role in processing financial transactions and managing the counterparty default risks in those transactions. In other words, the CCP is a risk manager for the clearing members. This system allows the clearing members to be protected against a default by any of the other clearing members. But how is a CCP protected against the default of one or more clearing members? The first level of protection is the mechanism of a waterfall whose resources are provided predominantly by the clearing members. With this mechanism, a CCP should be able to survive the default of its two largest clearing members.

However, this cannot prevent the waterfall mechanism from being inadequate in the event of a large crisis. If such a crisis should spread to a CCP, normal insolvency procedures may not provide sufficient tools to intervene within an appropriate timeframe. This is especially the case when the measures undertaken by the CCP during the recovery phase have failed to restore a matched book and cover the losses caused by the default event. In this case, it is necessary to have a special applicable resolution framework for CCPs to avoid negative repercussions for the financial system.

The resolution of a CCP would not be an isolated event. It would likely only occur in connection with huge market turmoil, including the resolution of several clearing members as a prerequisite, because the CCP's resolution would

Levin Holle, Head of Financial Markets Policy Department, German Federal Ministry of Finance

https://doi.org/10.1515/9783110644067-018

only be necessary if the recovery or resolution of the clearing members had not been successful. Such a situation would be unprecedented for CCPs and its supervisors. In addition to risks from default losses, CCPs are subject to risks from non-default losses. These are losses stemming from, for example, fraud, operational risks or cyber-attacks.

To achieve an effective resolution plan, the selection of appropriate resolution tools is essential. It must also be ensured that the resolution mechanisms are efficient for regulators or the resolution authorities and for market participants in such exceptional circumstances.

Within this framework, it is crucial to distinguish between default and non-default losses. Default losses are caused if the default of clearing members cannot be covered by the waterfall alone. In this case, the risk of default comes from the clearing members. So the conclusion should be that clearing members as a risk community have to bear the losses first, because CCPs are not the risk-takers and the functions of CCPs do not include being exposed to market risks. In the case of non-default losses, we can in general suppose that management or other faults within the sphere of responsibility of the CCP's board have occurred, so that the owners of the CCP have to bear losses first in this case.

With such a framework, one could keep the function of a CCP alive as long as is necessary to avoid negative repercussions for the whole financial system and the wider economy. That is the reason why the European Commission published in November 2016 a draft regulation concerning recovery and resolution of CCPs (COM (2016) 856 final, 2016/0365, dated 28. 11. 2016), which also transposes most of the FSB's proposals, which were published in July 2017 in its guidance on Central Counterparty Resolution and Resolution Planning. On the EU level, the negotiations are still ongoing.

2 Impact of resolution planning and compatibility of certain resolution tools with CCPs' business models

In principle, a CCP's waterfall comprises either one single default fund for all product classes or single default funds for each product class cleared by a CCP with the option that losses from an exhausted single default fund could be covered by another single default fund. It is often claimed that the model with several individual default funds could isolate risks and lead to a resolution of only that critical default fund, thereby avoiding the complete resolution of the CCP. Such a segregation of products in special default funds may not be complete and have negative effects. It derogates from some of the benefits which were the initial reason for introducing central clearing e.g. netting and margining efficiency, and it may interfere with current risk models and concepts of risk diversification.

However, if the CCP requests the introduction of a special waterfall for each product class, risks related to the resolution of a CCP might be reduced. Under such circumstances, the CCP might have the chance to limit the consequences of a default or non-default event to the product class where the probable first losses caused by the event are located.

In an extreme crisis, such a model might not be able to reduce the resolution risk for a CCP. In such a crisis, it is very likely that defaulting clearing members would indeed suffer extreme losses in relation to all or many of the product classes cleared by the CCP. In the end, all the individual default funds of a CCP could suffer losses which could not be covered. So the probable result would be a resolution of the whole CCP. Taking into account the possibility of an extreme crisis, it might be more appropriate to allow the resolution authority to only split up waterfalls along product classes to facilitate the resolution of a CCP.

Certain resolution tools like termination of contracts, variation margin haircutting or a special resolution cash calls are broadly in line with the business model of CCPs. Extending the tool box and incorporating an obligation for the CCP to issue special bail-in instruments as special corporate bonds might be at odds with CCPs' risk specifics.

3 Additional own funds, second tranche of skin in the game

Additional equity and/or a second tranche of skin in the game could be helpful in covering a CCP's losses stemming from a default or a non-default event. In this respect, the distinction between a default and a non-default event as the reason for the resolution of a CCP could help to determine whether the clearing members or the CCP or its shareholders should cover the losses first.

If a default of clearing members causes the crisis it seems to be justified if the clearing members as a risk community do cover the losses first. Here the core role and function of a CCP has to be recognized. A CCP is the circuit breaker which helps to mutualize and spread the effects of a default of one or more clearing members. CCPs manage risks coming from individual or multiple clearing members and transfer these risks through mutualisation. By doing so, a CCP stops contagion and dilutes the impact of the default of one or more clearing members on the overall system. A CCP's equity is small in comparison to the funds provided by these clearing members and the volume of risks the CCP has to manage. In this respect, the equity of the CCP alone will not be adequate to cover large losses. Therefore it is justified that the community of the clearing members bears the losses first. However more skin in the game reduces the conflict of interest between the owners or the shareholders of the CCP which do profit from its business and the clearing members who bear the losses in the case of the CCPs' resolution.

In most cases involving a non-default event, the CCP has control over the risks (for example fraud, operational risks or cyber-attacks) and should therefore be responsible for the losses, so that the CCP's shareholders should in principle cover these losses. Here the write down of equity is appropriate to cover losses in the event of the resolution of a CCP. Alternatively one could fix a certain amount to be paid by the shareholders of the CCP in the case of a non-default event, or the CCP could issue special bail-in-tools. Such measures in the case of a non-default seem to be justified if the CCP itself, its management or shareholders are responsible for the losses which caused the resolution. However if the resources of the owners or shareholders of the CCP are not sufficient to cover the losses in the case of a non-default, the default fund of the waterfall has to step in. That is justified simply to maintain the CCP's services, including in particular a matched book. In this respect, the clearing members have to cover the losses in their own interest.

In this context, one question remains: Could a second tranche of skin in the game be regarded as an incentive for robust risk management by the CCP? Indeed, the second tranche of skin in the game could be regarded as an additional incentive for robust risk management by the CCP and less as a loss absorption tool in the event of a default of clearing members. This could be justified because the CCP is only a risk manager and the clearing members are the risk-takers. It also needs to be clarified to what extent a second tranche of skin in the game should be introduced. The simplest way would be to enlarge the minimum equity as stipulated in EMIR.

4 Relations between the resolution of banks and CPPs

ESMA's second EU-wide stress test, conducted in 2017 and published on 2nd February 2018 (ESMA70-151–1154) shows that the system of EU CCPs appears to be resilient to multiple defaults of clearing members and extreme market shocks. The stress test examines systemically critical concentration of single clearing members or groups at EU-wide level. The interconnectedness between CCPs through common clearing members, custodians and liquidity providers has also been examined.

The results of the stress test do show that a severe crisis among the largest clearing members, which are often clearing members in more than one CCP, is likely to cause difficulties among the largest CCPs. Hence careful management of the recovery or resolution of clearing members if they are banks is a key factor in avoiding a crisis at one or more CCPs. Therefore, it is of utmost importance that the bank resolution authorities do ensure that a bank in resolution fulfils its obligations with regard to the CCPs it belongs to, if the bank in resolution is a clearing member. If these obligations are fulfilled, it may make it less likely that a CCP will have to undergo resolution in a severe crisis.

Otherwise a situation would occur, where the banking resolution authorities' prevention and resolution measures from their own regulatory regimes did not work and that cooperation between all kinds of bank authorities did not work either to avoid the stage where the resources dedicated to a CCP are in danger. In other words, the resolution authorities and supervisors that are responsible for the defaulted bank(s) would not have been able to prevent spreading the crisis across one or more CCPs. To avoid such a situation, close cooperation and involvement of resolution authorities and supervisors on a cross border basis is required. Such extended cross-border cooperation must not only ensure the management of the resolution of a CCP, but also the multiple resolutions of defaulting clearing members. Therefore it would be a mistake to believe that any resolution can be managed locally without taking into account the broader market or other jurisdictions.

5 Access to central bank liquidity

In the EU, some CCPs do have a banking license. With regard to the principles of the Eurosystem, access is granted if the CCPs are financially sound. In this respect, CCPs with a banking license have to fulfil the conditions stipulated by the Guideline of the ECB on the Eurosystem. The Eurosystem can impose sanctions on CCPs with a banking license which fail to comply with their obligations. The most important sanction is the suspension from open market operations or standing facilities.

On the other hand, CCPs without a banking license do not have the possibility of gaining access to general Eurosystem facilities. To avoid drawing on credit facilities or liquidity assistance by the Eurosystem, it is essential that the recovery plans as well as the resolution plans of the CCPs are operable. The plans should describe how their application can avoid assistance by the Eurosystem becoming necessary.

However in the event of a crisis the application of the resolution tools may be not sufficient to cover the losses. Furthermore, this might lead to liquidity shortfalls for the CCP. In such a critical situation, the Eurosystem itself has to decide whether it allows liquidity support or not. This decision has to be taken bearing in mind the guaranteed independence of the central banks.

6 Shareholders vs. clearing members and their clients, compensation of clearing members

It is often discussed that if a CCP in recovery has applied position and loss allocation tools to non-defaulting clearing members and the CCP has not entered into resolution, these clearing members should receive compensation for their losses. This raises the question of whether compensation of clearing members could in general represent an incentive to participate in the recovery and resolution process. Furthermore it could be justified to distinguish within such a process between whether the CCP crisis has been caused by a default of clearing members or by a non-default event. This distinction could be important if clearing members have covered losses in the case of a non-default event.

The rule books of the CCPs do stipulate that clearing members have to participate in the recovery process of a CCP, especially to cover losses caused by a default of one or more clearing members. Comparable procedures for loss allocation are part of the resolution planning. If non-defaulting clearing members do suffer losses in resolution, the question of whether they may receive compensation is currently under discussion. Some argue that in the case of a default, as well as in the case of a non-default, the CCP should compensate the clearing members for their loss through cash payments or instruments of ownership securitizing future profits of the CCP. The clearing members do compose a risk community which is obliged to apply the rule book, other contractual stipulations and the resolution plan to cover allocated losses of the CCP in the case of a default event. Therefore the non-defaulting clearing members should in general fulfil their obligations without compensation from the CCP.

V Conclusion

Paul Tucker

Resolution policy and systemic risk: Five entreaties

Perhaps the bigget lesson of the Great Financial Crisis was that it is a very big mistake to focus regulatory policy almost exclusively on reducing the *probability* of financial intermediaries failing. Looking back, this long-standing mindset is truly bizarre given the habitual refrain of prudential supervisors (and their political overseers) that they do not aim for zero failures. That being so, it is absolutely vital also to focus on containing the impact of intermediaries' distress and failure.

While the United States went into the crisis with an effective resolution regime for small and medium-sized deposit-takers, few other G7 countries did. And even the US did not have a resolution regime that could cope with the failure of large and complex banking groups or of those non-banks whose bankruptcy would exacerbate systemic spillovers.[1]

Perhaps the most profound shift in high policy following the disaster of 2008/09, therefore, is the effort to give resolution policy equal standing with prophylactic regulation and supervision. If that was the goal, however, it has not yet been achieved. While the United States has done a lot more than most of its peers to implement internationally agreed policy on resolution, it has not done nearly as much as it could have. And while the EU has a strong statutory framework – possibly better than the US's – its implementation has to date been flawed.

Against that background, I will briefly make five points, which amount to a series of entreaties to current policy makers. They concern: the need to be careful when claiming that Too Big To Fail has been "solved"; how resolution policy can lift a burden from the Lender of Last Resort; how prudential supervisors need to be more prescriptive about the structure of banking groups; how resolution policy can hard wire cross-border cooperation; and how it could help contain a full blown systemic crisis in which many intermediaries were falling over more or less simultaneously.[2]

---

1 Amazingly, the lack of such tools had been made clear in the early-2000s in an unpublished report to the then Financial Stability Forum and G10. Disclosure: I was a member of the working group.

2 This draws on Tucker, "Resolution Policy and Resolvability at the Centre of Financial Stability Regimes?" IADI/BIS FSI conference, Basel, 1 February 2018. http://paultucker.me/wp-content/uploads/2018/04/Resolution-Policy-And-Resolvability.pdf

---

Paul Tucker, Chair, Systemic Risk Council, and Harvard Kennedy School

https://doi.org/10.1515/9783110644067-019

The hazards in claiming to have "solved" too big to fail

Policymakers have become fond of suggesting that they have solved the problem of Too Big to Fail (TBTF). There is some truth in this, but the claim can also mislead anyone not intimately involved. I will try to distinguish the wheat from the chaff.

The sense in which it is true is that more jurisdictions are now approaching the position that, in October 2013, shortly before leaving office, I said the US had already reached[3]:

> I cannot see how the US Administration could persuade Congress to provide taxpayer solvency support to – ie bailout – some of the biggest US banks and dealers. In short, the US authorities have the technology – via Title II of Dodd Frank; and, just as important, most US bank and dealer groups are, through an accident of history, organised in way that lends them to top-down resolution on a group-wide basis. I don't mean it would be completely smooth right now; it would be smoother in a year or so as more progress is made. But in extremis, it could be done now.

But the statement that Too Big to Fail has been solved is misleading if understood as meaning or implying that no firm's distress could ever, in any circumstances, cause economic dislocation and other social costs.

In the past, when faced with an ailing large and complex firm, the authorities felt they had to choose between, on the one hand, putting the firm into a regular bankruptcy proceeding and accepting massive systemic disorder and, on the other hand, a taxpayer bailout to avert systemic collapse. That is no longer so.

When a giant firm fails, there will be nasty spill overs. But using the resolution strategies described below, it should be possible for the social pain to be contained sufficiently for government bailout not to be the *only* sane policy response. That will be achieved if resolution can ensure that essential services to the real economy (payments transfers, credit supply, risk transfer) are tolerably maintained. Indeed, preserving the flow of essential services should be thought of as the objective.

3 Paul Tucker: Solving too big to fail – where do things stand on resolution?

Speech by Paul Tucker, Deputy Governor, Bank of England, at the Institute of International Finance 2013 Annual Membership meeting, Washington DC, 12 October 2013. The 'accident of history' referred to is that, as a result of a long-repealed bar on inter-state banking, most significant US banking groups comprise operating companies owned by a pure holding company that does not itself provide services to households or businesses.

The acid test of whether that objective has been achieved is whether elected politicians *do feel compelled* to bail out equity holders and bondholders. If they do, the banking system is semi-socialised, which would continue to fuel popular discontent. On that basis, the Italian bailouts during 2018 were a clear (and avoidable) policy failure.

In summary, my first entreaty is that policymakers should take care to explain that resolution of massive firms will contain distress but not eliminate it. The public needs to know that our economies need not revisit the barely controlled mess of 2008, but understand that banking failures will not be painless.

Transformation for the lender of last resort

Once credible resolution regimes and plans are in place, a *fatally* wounded firm should not be propped up by lender-of-last-resort (LOLR) assistance from the central bank. This matters to the legitimacy of independent central banks because critics allege, fairly or unfairly, that some, including the Federal Reserve, overstepped the mark in the past.[4]

If a firm is fundamentally bust, there should be no question of liquidity assistance from the central bank. Similarly, if the condition of an initially solvent firm deteriorates after LOLR support has been extended to the point where it is fundamentally insolvent, the central bank should withdraw its support and put the firm into resolution. Of course sometimes liquidity assistance can restore an ailing firm to health, and liquidity assistance to the system as a whole can sometimes lift asset prices and avoid economic collapse, levitating distressed firms back to life. So by "fundamentally bust" I mean that there is no realistically plausible path for the economy and, hence, for the firm's asset portfolio under which it will be able to repay its debts as they fall due.

The vital distinction between fundamentally sound and unsound borrowers for LOLR policy arises because time-subordination exists while a firm is alive

---

4 Whether or not it is true, that is levelled at the Fed by various authors (who reach different normative judgments). See, for example, Humphrey Thomas M. "Lender of Last Resort: What It Is, Whence It Came, and Why the Fed Isn't It." *Cato Journal* 30, no. 2 (2010): 333–64; Posner, Eric, "What Legal Authority Does the Fed Need during a Financial Crisis?" University of Chicago Public Law Working Paper, no. 560, February 3, 2016; Wallach, Philip. *To the Edge: Legality, Legitimacy, and the Response to the 2008 Financial Crisis*. Washington, DC: Brookings Institution Press, 2015.

but not when in bankruptcy.[5] In consequence, liquidity assistance to a fundamentally bust bank allows short-term creditors to be repaid at the expense of long-term creditors of the same rank. It is not for unelected central bankers to play God in that way, side-stepping the long-standing policy preferences embedded in bankruptcy law.

"But we are playing God if we let firms fail," some might answer. Whatever one thinks about how they handled that dilemma in the past, they can escape it now. Credible resolution plans for handling irretrievably bankrupt firms makes it credible for the LOLR to say 'no'.

This regime change does not preclude central banks providing *post-resolution* liquidity assistance to firms that have been restored to solvency and viability (as well as to innocent bystanders).

More central banks need to make all this clear in public statements of their LOLR principles, which they should discuss much more than in the past. The doctrine of "constructive ambiguity", a casual refrain for so many years, was a mistake.[6]

Resolvability through structure: Reorienting prudential supervisors

Given the shift in high policy I have described, it is essential that prudential supervisors focus not only on reducing the probability of failure. They must also work backwards from insolvency and lack of viability, ensuring that distress, when it occurs, does not entail taxpayer bailout or a systemic crisis.

5 When a firm is alive, long-term claims fall due after maturing short-term claims, exposing long-term creditors to the risk that the firm deteriorates before their claims approach maturity: this is time-subordination. Upon entry into bankruptcy, however, things are different. Some debt claims are accelerated by their contractual terms and, more generally, liquidators are not permitted to pay out to short-term creditors if longer term creditors of the same seniority would be left worse off as a result: their claims rank *pari passu*. On the "no lending to fundamentally unsound firms" precept and the insufficiency of good collateral, see *Unelected Power*, chapter 23, and Tucker, "The Lender of Last Resort and Modern Central Banking: Principles and Reconstruction." BIS Papers, No. 79, Bank for International Settlements, 2014.

6 For the ECB, see Yves Mersch, "The Limits of Central Bank Financing in Resolution," European Central Bank, 30 January 2018. Also, Bank of England, *Approach to Resolution*, October 2017, page 22. It matters at what point in the resolution process the Window should become available: it should be once the LOLR is satisfied that the operating company has been restored to solvency, not when all the formalities, which might take months, are complete.

A sound statutory resolution regime, with a wide range of powers, is necessary but not sufficient. It is equally necessary to reorient supervisors towards ensuring that groups and firms are resolvable using those powers. That was the plan. Things have been done but it is, at best, work in progress. So my entreaty here is to redouble action on this front.

The key initiative must be mandating corporate structures – legal and financial – that enable resolution tools to be used in a way that can keep distressed operating companies going while imposing losses on subordinated creditors. The utility of the so-called bail-in instrument depends on corporate structure, as I described back in 2013[7]:

> The Single Point of Entry versus Multiple Point of Entry resolution strategy distinction may be the most important innovation in banking policy in decades
>
> We will learn to speak of banks and dealers as either "SPE groups" or "MPE groups". Some technical developments don't matter hugely. This one does.
>
> A single-point-of-entry or SPE resolution works downwards from the group's top company – most simply, a pure holding company (Holdco). Losses in subsidiaries are first transferred up to Holdco. If Holdco is bankrupt as a result, the group needs resolving. The "bailin" tool is applied to Holdco, with the equity being written off and bonds converted as necessary into equity to recapitalise the group. Those bondholders become the new owners. The group stays together.
>
> Under multiple-point-of-entry or MPE resolutions, by contrast, a group would be split up into some of its parts. Healthy parts might be sold or be maintained as a residual group shorn of their distressed sister companies. The resolution of the distressed parts might be effected via bailin of bonds that had been issued to the market by a regional intermediate holding company. . .
>
> For many financial groups, it is fairly obvious which broad resolution strategy (SPE or MPE) they are currently most suited to. But few major groups will escape having to make significant changes to their legal, organisational and financial structure to remove obstacles to effective resolution under that preferred strategy. . .
>
> For "MPE groups", many will need to do more to organise themselves into well-defined regional and functional subgroups, perhaps with regional or functional intermediate holding companies, which could be subjected to SPE resolutions. And these groups will need to ensure that common services, such as IT, are provided by stand-alone entities under contracts that are robust enough to survive the break up of the group.

Enshrined and promulgated via the Financial Stability Board's *Key Attributes of Effective Resolution Regimes*, endorsed by G20 leaders in 2011, this regime shift

7 Tucker, "Solving Too Big To Fail: Where Do Things Stand on Resolution?", Bank of England, October 2013.

generated a need for minimum required levels of *gone-concern* loss-absorbing capacity (colloquially, bail-inable bonds).[8] The FSB delivered that through its requirements for total loss-absorbing capacity (TLAC).

I have two specific entreaties.

'Inside' versus 'outside' loss-absorbing capacity

The first concerns who holds the bonds that would fall to be bailed-in immediately after equity is extinguished. If contagion is to be contained, this very obviously matters. Holders should not include other banks or bank-like entities such as money market mutual funds: otherwise, the monetary system would have only 'inside' loss-absorbing capacity, which is of no use at all in protecting the system as whole.

But that policy cannot be enough. Longer-term investment institutions, such as life insurance companies and pension funds, should be subject to aggregate exposure limits to such instruments. And retail investors must be warned that they are risky: exactly what did not happen in Italy, despite their officials being alerted to this years ago.

We should be concerned, then, that G20 policy statements do not go further than saying that there should be limits on the biggest firms and other internationally active banks holding each other's TLAC instruments; and that the implementation in some jurisdictions, including the EU, is arguably weaker still.[9] This leaves open the incentive of bankers to distribute bonds issued by global banks and by domestically significant firms to medium-sized domestic banks and money funds, a likely (and crazy) recipe for contagion from distressed global firms to domestic financial systems. Similarly, it gives banks incentives to sell their bonds to retail investors, an equally reckless recipe for political pressure to resort to bailouts rather than bail-ins.

8 The term 'bail-inable bonds' is a convenient but misleading shorthand. Whether something can be bailed-in as a matter of law is simply a question of the resolution authority's statutory powers. Whether it is sensible to do so given the public policy objective depends on the firm and group's capital structure. This is not about term sheets and financial engineering. A recent G30 report gets in muddle over this: p.10 of Group of 30, "Managing the Next Financial Crisis," 2018.

9 Financial Stability Board, 2015, Total Loss-Absorbing Capacity (TLAC) Principles and Term Sheet, November, Principle (xii). http://www.fsb.org/2015/11/total-loss-absorbing-capacity-tlac-principles-and-term-sheet/

Prescribing the ranking of opco creditors

My second entreaty to prudential supervisors concerns the creditor hierarchy of operating banks and dealers. It requires a second round of fundamental policy initiatives.

In my description of SPE-resolution groups (and MPE-resolution groups), I assumed that the bonds to be bailed in were issued by a pure holding company (or, for MPE-groups, intermediate subgroup holdcos), and so were structurally subordinated. Many current and former policymakers, including myself, prefer structural subordination, but it is not an international standard or, more important, universally applied.

Where subordination is delivered either by legislation (Germany) or contract (France), it is the external creditors of the operating entity that will be haircut when it fails, which I expect to pose formidable communication difficulties for the authorities as they will have to explain why a firm is sound even though it is in intensive care. Be that as it may, however, resolution authorities *everywhere* cannot rely 100% on the first layer of required bailin-able bonds sufficing in every single case to absorb losses and recapitalize a distressed firm. When, eventually, that proves not to be the case, the authorities concerned will be faced with haircutting other creditors or, alternatively, providing fiscal support to the ailing firm after equity holders and subordinated bondholders have been wiped out.

At present, in some jurisdictions the resolution authority is permitted to distinguish between creditors that, formally, would rank equally in bankruptcy if it judges that differential treatment is necessary to maintain financial stability (or contain instability). This is not infrequently objected to on the grounds that it cuts across our rule-of-law values of fairness and predictability. The trade-off is clear enough. Either resolution authorities (and bankruptcy judges) need to be able to exercise discretion in the pursuit of a clear statutory objective to contain instability; or legislators and/or regulatory authorities need to be much more prescriptive about the permissible creditor hierarchy so that the need for any such discrimination is eliminated.

In Europe, this is the background to legislators having made insured depositors (and the deposit insurance scheme) preferred creditors. But more granular prescriptions would prove to have been needed if ever a large and complex operating company goes into resolution. For example, is it really sensible for trade creditors (for example, the people who supply food and transport services to banks) to rank equally with senior bondholders? Should there be a distinction between wholesale deposits that are short-term and long term? Where should derivative counterparty-credit exposures come?

I am not going to offer specific proposals here. Instead, I want to underline that those who argue *against* resolution agencies exercising discretion should also be arguing *for* greater regulation of bank and dealer creditor hierarchies. That is a hole in policy on both sides of the Atlantic.[10]

Hard wiring cross-border cooperation

I still occasionally hear current and former policymakers saying that the biggest challenge during a resolution will be cross-border cooperation. I find this baffling given the policy debates and agreements that were, and I believe remain, central to the post-crisis reform programme.

The plans I summarized for SPE-style resolutions were designed to – and *can* – solve the challenges in the cross-border resolution of international banking groups. In essence, the solution is for overseas (and domestic) opco subsidiaries to issue super-subordinated debt to their parent group/sub-group holdco, with *host* authorities being able to trigger write down (or conversion into equity) whenever they would otherwise be empowered to put the subsidiary into a local resolution or bankruptcy process.[11]

Those subordinated intra-group bonds become known as Internal TLAC.[12] Writing them down/converting them into equity enables losses exceeding a foreign subsidiary's equity to be transmitted up to the home country holding company (or intermediate holdco), without the local subsidiary itself going into default. If as a result the foreign holding company is mortally wounded, that is for the group's home authorities, and for them alone, to sort out.

Thus, careful specification of the trigger for "converting" intra-group debt into equity can hard-wire co-operation between the home and host authorities. This requires open and frank discussions. When planning for resolvability, home and host authorities might fail to agree, for any one of a number of

---

10 The gap exists in, for example, the report by the US Treasury: US Department of the Treasury, *Orderly Liquidation Authority and Bankruptcy Reform* (Feb. 2018), *available at* https://home.treasury.gov/sites/default/files/2018-02/OLA_REPORT.pdf.

11 For a post-office account of the analysis underpinning the new resolution policies, see P Tucker, 'The Resolution of Financial Institutions without Taxpayer Solvency Support: Seven Retrospective Clarifications and Elaborations', European Summer Symposium in Economic Theory, Gerzensee, Switzerland, 3 July 2014.

12 Financial Stability Board, 2015, Total Loss-Absorbing Capacity (TLAC) Principles and Term Sheet, November. http://www.fsb.org/2015/11/total-loss-absorbing-capacity-tlac-principles-and-term-sheet/

reasons, that intra-group gone-concern loss-absorbing bonds must be issued by an opco subsidiary to its foreign holdco, For example, home authorities might worry that a host would be trigger happy. On the other side, it cannot be ruled out that a host supervisor would conclude that their local subsidiary would be unviable on a stand-alone basis even if clearly solvent, but that the group's home authorities are not capable of delivering a top-down resolution of the group as a whole. In either of those (and other) circumstances, home and host authorities would be discovering *ex ante* that they cannot rely on each other.

The problem having been brought to the surface, it would need to be confronted up front. To make its business resolvable, any such group would need to be broken up in some fashion or restructured into ring-fenced silos (for MPE resolution). However disappointing, that is much much better than host and home authorities discovering in the midst of an actual crisis that they cannot rely upon each other.

This should – and, to be clear, was definitely intended to – give a harder edge to discussions amongst home and host authorities, finally bringing real substance to supervisory and crisis-management colleges (whose members have had incentives to attest that they work better than, I suspect, independent observers or top policymakers believe).

The question is whether or not this kind of hard-edged engagement is what is going on. I am not convinced that what I have been describing, the very core of the FSB Key Attributes-led policy, has been gripped (or, perhaps, even understood) across the policy-making community.

My entreaty here, therefore, is that home and host authorities publish exactly where they have got to on each group designated as globally systemic.

What about a systemic crisis?

My final entreaty concerns what happens when a few, even a host of, systemically significant financial institutions (SIFIs) fail more or less simultaneously.[13] Critics of resolution policy say that in those circumstances governments are still going to bail out firms, and thus that not much has changed.

13 With some hindsight, it was a mistake to move from the pre-crisis term Large and Complex Financial Institution (LCFI) to Systemically Important Financial Institution (SIFI) as the latter invites the perception that SIFIs need to be bailed out by the taxpayer – a perception that critics have been keen to foster and embed in public opinion.

While this should obviously be taken seriously, we should not fall into a pessimism of absolutes.

In the first place, even if bail-in were to work only for idiosyncratic cases, it could still bring about a substantial change in market discipline, reducing the moral hazard that plagues finance.

Second, the critics are wrong to say that bail-in must entail contagion. If the structural policies I have described are followed and if sufficient gone-concern loss-absorbing capacity exists, applying bail-in would not directly create disorder through the financial system's inter-connectedness. That is because operating banks would not go into bankruptcy or resolution, and investors in the bailed-in holdco bonds would be longer-term or unlevered investment vehicles with limited aggregate exposures. I would entreat critics to descend from generalisations and look at how far jurisdictions are (or are not) pursuing some of the necessary supporting policies I have summarised.

Third, the perfectly valid (and obvious) point that executing bail-in would be more difficult during a fully fledged systemic crisis does not mean that elected politicians should deliberately, by design, be left with no option other than to bail out bondholders and equity holders. That would be to repeat the tragic mistakes of pre-crisis policymakers.

An alternative would be for central government politicians to have the power to apply bail-in across the board to as many distressed firms as necessary. This power would have to be exercised *before* every afflicted firm had reached the point of non-viability (PONV) relevant for a stand-alone bail-in. It would involve bondholders, not taxpayers, recapitalising the system.

I am not saying that executive government could confidently be relied upon to deploy multiple-firm bail-in rather than bailout. Nor am I asserting that there is a zero chance of fiscal measures being needed at some point in the future.[14] But the frontier at which taxpayers come to the rescue in order to keep the financial system going can be shifted outwards. In terms of incentives, it would be useful, moreover, to put politicians in a position where they have to account *ex post* for actively choosing bailout rather than other crisis-management tools available to them.

So my final entreaty is to take systemic crises seriously rather than as an opportunity for making debating points. Although not discussed here, I take that to be the spirit of Mervyn King's proposal that all the short-term liabilities

14 A point stressed by former US Treasury Secretary Geithner, who very much continues to focus on the inevitability of extemporizing in the face of unimagined disasters. Geithner, Timothy, "Are We Safer? The Case for Updating Bagehot." 2016 Per Jacobsson Lecture, The Per Jacobsson Foundation.

of banks should be covered by assets that can be used as collateral at the central bank.[15] My proposal is complementary as liquidity cannot bring back to life fundamentally insolvent firms, only (sometimes) the innocent bystanders.

Conclusions

Experience surely makes it clear that a resilient financial system cannot be delivered only by trying to avoid firms failing, the traditional focus of prudential supervisors. Instead, a decent system will be able to cope with failure, containing the social costs of financial firms' distress when it inevitably occurs. That belated realization was at the very centre of post-crisis policy. But it has yet to achieve the prominence it badly needs in public debate.

In this essay, I have made a series of entreaties. They are that:

1) Policymakers should take care to explain that effective resolution of massive firms really will contain distress but will not eliminate it.
2) Central banks should publish how the availability of credible resolution regimes has changed the way they will operate LOLR policies.
3) Prudential supervisors and securities regulators should be more prescriptive about who can hold financial groups' bail-inable debt, and about the permissible creditor hierarchy of operating companies supplying important financial services.
4) Home and host authorities should announce for every systemically significant financial group whether they have reached agreement on local subsidiaries issuing to their foreign parent bonds that the host could write down or convert into equity; and how they plan to restructure any groups for which they have not reached such an agreement.
5) Policymakers should explore what new resolution powers for the executive branch might help to avoid taxpayer bailouts in a systemic crisis with multiple firms in distress simultaneously.

15 Mervyn King, *End of Alchemy*, chapter 7, pp. 269–281. An idea of this kind was first floated in the Bank of England when, before the Great Financial Crisis, we were thinking about contingency plans for a 9/11-type disaster. I describe how the idea could be operationalized in Tucker, Paul (2018), "Is the financial system sufficiently resilient? A research and policy agenda on informationally insensitive 'safe' assets within a money-credit constitution", BIS Working Papers, forthcoming.

Of course that is not the beginning and end of crisis-management policy. We also need to know, for example, how supervisors will use the time provided by central banks' liquidity assistance to make banks and other intermediaries deleverage before it is too late: a missed opportunity during the 2007/08 crisis on which we are no wiser.

But effective resolution policy is within the grasp of the authorities, and needs to be completed. Those interested in a stable financial system have got to generate as much discussion and media coverage of resolution policy as already exists for the more familiar parts of banking supervision. The thing about avoidable mistakes is that they can and should be avoided.

Kolibri 360 GmbH
Ferdinand-Jühlke-Straße 7
99095 Erfurt, Deutschland
produktsicherheit@kolibri360.de